OPPOSING
VIEWPOINTS®
SERIES

Energy Alternatives

D1057604

Other Books of Related Interest:

Opposing Viewpoints Series

The Environment

Global Resources

Oil

Current Controversies Series

Alternative Energy Sources

Conserving the Environment

Pollution

At Issue Series

Foreign Oil Dependence

Is the World Heading to an Energy Crisis?

Nuclear and Toxic Waste

"Congress shall make no law . . . abridging the freedom of speech, or of the press."

First Amendment to the U.S. Constitution

The basic foundation of our democracy is the First Amendment guarantee of freedom of expression. The Opposing Viewpoints Series is dedicated to the concept of this basic freedom and the idea that it is more important to practice it than to enshrine it.

OPPOSING
VIEWPOINTS®
SERIES

Energy Alternatives

Barbara Passero, Book Editor

GREENHAVEN PRESS

An imprint of Thomson Gale, a part of The Thomson Corporation

THOMSON

™

GALE

Detroit • New York • San Francisco • New Haven, Conn. • Waterville, Maine • London

Christine Nasso, *Publisher*
Elizabeth Des Chenes, *Managing Editor*

© 2006 Thomson Gale, a part of The Thomson Corporation.

Thomson and Star logo are trademarks and Gale and Greenhaven Press are registered trademarks used herein under license.

For more information, contact:
Greenhaven Press
27500 Drake Rd.
Farmington Hills, MI 48331-3535
Or you can visit our Internet site at http://www.gale.com

LIBRARY OF CONGRESS CATALOGING-IN-PUBLICATION DATA

Energy Alternatives / Barbara Passero, book editor.
    p. cm. -- (Opposing viewpoints)
    Includes bibliographical references and index.
    ISBN-13: 978-0-7377-3350-1 (lib. hardcover : alk. paper)
    ISBN-10: 0-7377-3350-0 (lib. hardcover : alk. paper)
    ISBN-13: 978-0-7377-3351-8 (pbk. : alk. paper)
    ISBN-10: 0-7377-3351-9 (pbk. : alk. paper)
    1. Renewable energy sources--Juvenile literature. I. Passero, Barbara.
    TJ808.2.E628 2006
    333.79--dc22

                      2006022293

Printed in the United States of America
10 9 8 7 6 5 4 3 2 1

Contents

Chapter 3: What Renewable Energy Sources Should Be Developed?

Why Consider
Opposing Viewpoints?

"The only way in which a human being can make some approach to knowing the whole of a subject is by hearing what can be said about it by persons of every variety of opinion and studying all modes in which it can be looked at by every character of mind. No wise man ever acquired his wisdom in any mode but this."

John Stuart Mill

In our media-intensive culture it is not difficult to find differing opinions. Thousands of newspapers and magazines and dozens of radio and television talk shows resound with differing points of view. The difficulty lies in deciding which opinion to agree with and which "experts" seem the most credible. The more inundated we become with differing opinions and claims, the more essential it is to hone critical reading and thinking skills to evaluate these ideas. Opposing Viewpoints books address this problem directly by presenting stimulating debates that can be used to enhance and teach these skills. The varied opinions contained in each book examine many different aspects of a single issue. While examining these conveniently edited opposing views, readers can develop critical thinking skills such as the ability to compare and contrast authors' credibility, facts, argumentation styles, use of persuasive techniques, and other stylistic tools. In short, the Opposing Viewpoints Series is an ideal way to attain the higher-level thinking and reading skills so essential in a culture of diverse and contradictory opinions.

In addition to providing a tool for critical thinking, Opposing Viewpoints books challenge readers to question their own strongly held opinions and assumptions. Most people form their opinions on the basis of upbringing, peer pressure, and personal, cultural, or professional bias. By reading carefully balanced opposing views, readers must directly confront new ideas as well as the opinions of those with whom they disagree. This is not to simplistically argue that everyone who reads opposing views will—or should—change his or her opinion. Instead, the series enhances readers' understanding of their own views by encouraging confrontation with opposing ideas. Careful examination of others' views can lead to the readers' understanding of the logical inconsistencies in their own opinions, perspective on why they hold an opinion, and the consideration of the possibility that their opinion requires further evaluation.

Evaluating Other Opinions

To ensure that this type of examination occurs, Opposing Viewpoints books present all types of opinions. Prominent spokespeople on different sides of each issue as well as well-known professionals from many disciplines challenge the reader. An additional goal of the series is to provide a forum for other, less known, or even unpopular viewpoints. The opinion of an ordinary person who has had to make the decision to cut off life support from a terminally ill relative, for example, may be just as valuable and provide just as much insight as a medical ethicist's professional opinion. The editors have two additional purposes in including these less known views. One, the editors encourage readers to respect others' opinions—even when not enhanced by professional credibility. It is only by reading or listening to and objectively evaluating others' ideas that one can determine whether they are worthy of consideration. Two, the inclusion of such viewpoints encourages the important critical thinking skill of objectively evaluating an author's credentials and bias. This evaluation will illuminate an author's reasons for taking a particular stance on an issue and will aid in readers' evaluation of the author's ideas.

It is our hope that these books will give readers a deeper understanding of the issues debated and an appreciation of the complexity of even seemingly simple issues when good and honest people disagree. This awareness is particularly important in a democratic society such as ours in which people enter into public debate to determine the common good. Those with whom one disagrees should not be regarded as enemies but rather as people whose views deserve careful examination and may shed light on one's own.

Thomas Jefferson once said that "difference of opinion leads to inquiry, and inquiry to truth." Jefferson, a broadly educated man, argued that "if a nation expects to be ignorant and free . . . it expects what never was and never will be." As individuals and as a nation, it is imperative that we consider the opinions of others and examine them with skill and discernment. The Opposing Viewpoints Series is intended to help readers achieve this goal.

David L. Bender and Bruno Leone,
Founders

Introduction

The modern world runs on oil. Most Americans know that their automobile gasoline and heating oil—essential to mobility and shelter—come from petroleum, but many do not realize how many other goods and services they depend on daily are also derived from petroleum: plastics, fertilizers and pesticides, paints, inks, medicines, roofing and road paving, fabric, telecommunication cable, and a host of other products from shampoo to candles to candy. Worldwide, petroleum products representing 80 million barrels of oil are consumed every day.

The largest share of that consumption takes place in the United States. Though Americans represent only 5 percent of the world's population, they consume an estimated 26 percent of the world's oil. Indeed the United States has long been the biggest consumer of all natural resources and as such the primary target of environmentalists and economists concerned about resource depletion. In discussion of the energy crisis, however, the United States is likely to be eclipsed as the world's biggest fossil-fuel consumer.

The new leader soon may be China, which has already surpassed the United States in consumption of grain, meat, coal, and steel, four of the five basic food, energy, and industrial commodities along with oil. According to Lester R. Brown of the Earth Policy Institute:

> With oil, the United States is still solidly in the lead with consumption triple that of China's—20.4 million barrels per day to 6.5 million barrels in 2004. But while oil use in the United States expanded by only 15 percent from 1994 to 2004, use in the new industrial giant more than doubled. Having recently eclipsed Japan as an oil consumer, China is now second only to the United States.

Looking at energy use in China means also considering coal, which supplies nearly two-thirds of energy demand. Here China's burning of 800 million tons easily exceeds the 574 million tons burned in the United States. With its coal use far exceeding that of the United States and with its oil and natural gas use climbing fast, it is only a matter of time until China will also be the world's top emitter of carbon. Soon the world may have two major climate disrupters. (Lester R. Brown, "China Replacing the United States as World's Leading Consumer," Earth Policy Institute, February 16, 2005. www.earth-policy.org/Updates/Update45.htm.)

China needs more oil (and every other raw material) to feed its booming economy. A nation of 1.3 billion people (compared with nearly 300 million people in the United States), China is setting a world-record pace in industrialization, rising personal income, and sale of consumer goods. Automobile sales double in China every two years, as do the number of computers in use. A striking example of China's explosive economic growth is seen in its communications industry: Between 1996 and 2003 the number of cell phones in the United States rose from 44 million to 159 million. During that same period, the number of cell phones in China rose from 7 million to 269 million.

China's domestic oil production satisfies only about two-thirds of its crude oil requirements, however, and as its demand for oil rises, so must its oil imports. China's economic policy has shifted accordingly, from protectionism to huge foreign investment and strategic partnerships with countries rich in oil, natural gas, and timber such as Russia, Brazil, and Indonesia. In June 2005 the China National Offshore Oil Corporation (CNOOC), an oil producer 70 percent owned by the Chinese government, offered to buy the major American oil company Unocal, which controls large reserves of oil in Asia. The CNOOC bid set off intense debate about political influence in the global oil market, and ultimately it was rejected, but the incident fed the public perception that competition for vital energy supplies is only going to intensify and may soon get nasty.

China is not the only rising economic power to put unprecedented demand on the world's remaining oil. India's economy is surging too, raising concerns about the subcontinent's ability to meet its energy needs, as journalist Praful Bidwai warned in March 2005:

India has shown a voracious, indeed monstrous, appetite for oil and gas as it burns increasing volumes of them in cars, two-wheelers, and to generate the electricity on which television sets, air conditioners and other gadgets fuelling the consumer boom run. In 2004 alone, India's oil consumption spurted by 11 per cent despite sky-high oil prices. India is now the world's fourth biggest oil consumer, following [the] U.S., China and Russia. . . .

India's oil consumption, now about 2.25 million bbl/day [barrels/day], is estimated to rise, at present rates of expansion, to a huge 5 million bbl in five to seven years. This should make all environmentally conscious citizens sick with anxiety. There is no way that India can or should sustain such high levels of energy consumption without causing enormous and irreversible damage to the global environment.

(Praful Bidwai, "India's Indigestible Oil Gulp," *Frontline*, March 12–25, 2005. www.hinduonnet.com/fline/fl2208/stories/20050422001810800.htm.)

The big question: Is there enough oil in the world to meet the growing need and growing competition for energy? Some analysts say yes, by using less (for example, by driving higher-mileage automobiles, installing better home insulation, and developing more efficient industrial processes) or producing more (for example, by opening more areas to oil drilling, increasing Persian Gulf oil production, and developing new technology to extract oil from oil shale). Others insist both of these strategies are temporary at best and predict dire economic and social consequences unless industrialized and rapidly industrializing nations quickly develop alternative sources of energy. The contributors to *Opposing Viewpoints: Energy Alternatives* debate whether the world can keep running on oil, and for how long, and what should take petroleum's place.

OPPOSING
VIEWPOINTS®
SERIES

CHAPTER 1

Are Alternative Energy Sources Necessary?

Chapter Preface

It is common knowledge that the earth's fossil fuels—petroleum, coal, and natural gas, formed in the ground from plant and animal remains over millions of years—are a finite resource. Just when the oil will run out, however, is the subject of heated debate. Understanding this disagreement depends on understanding the key concept known as peak oil, or the Hubbert peak theory.

The term *peak oil* comes from a paper presented to the American Petroleum Institute by American geophysicist Marion King Hubbert in 1956. Hubbert proposed a model of oil production and depletion that looks like a standard bell curve, plotting oil production against time. At point zero, oil reserves are discovered; oil production rises sharply as wells are drilled and the oil is pumped out. Much more oil remains in the ground than out of it. At some unspecified point, the curve reaches a peak that means half of the oil that will ever be produced has been taken out of the ground. From that point on, there is less and less oil in the ground than out of it; oil production inevitably declines and the curve falls until it approaches zero again.

Based on past production figures and calculations of known oil reserves at the time, Hubbert used this abstract model to predict that oil production would peak in the United States between 1965 and 1970, and worldwide in 1995. The Association for the Study of Peak Oil and Gas (ASPO) later adjusted Hubbert's worldwide peak estimate to 2004, reporting that the 30 billion barrels pumped that year equaled the remaining 30 billion barrels believed to exist underground.

Controversy arises over the date of peak oil because changing conditions continually force estimates to shift in one direction or the other. For example, the discovery of new oil fields, the development of new extraction methods that produce higher yields of oil, a sudden decline in human consumption, or the introduction of alternative energy sources all mean there is more oil available, and peak oil will occur further in the future. On the other hand, rapid economic and population growth boosts demand for oil, and the more oil production levels are raised to meet demand, the sooner peak oil will occur.

The uncertainty of these factors, and the interests of the agencies making peak oil predictions, contribute to a confusing variety of peak oil estimates. In 2005, for example, the ASPO revised its worldwide peak oil estimate to 2010, but the U.S. Geological Survey reports that there is enough oil to continue current production rates for fifty to a hundred years. In April 2006 a spokesman for Saudi Aramco, the world's leading crude oil producer, reported that production at its mature fields is now declining at a rate of 8 percent per year, and two of the three largest fields in the world, Mexico's Cantarell field and Kuwait's Burgan field, announced that they peaked in March 2006 and November 2005, respectively.

Amid rising gasoline prices, political instability in the oil-producing countries of the Middle East, and skyrocketing increases in demand for fossil fuels in developing economies, experts critique the peak oil model and debate the need for energy alternatives in the following chapter.

> *"[Oil depletion is] a problem of stagger-*
> *ing economic proportions . . . that could*
> *end up leading to more geopolitical fist-*
> *fights than you can ever imagine."*

The World Is Running Out of Oil

Matthew Simmons, interviewed by Amanda Griscom Little

Matthew Simmons, the conservative founder of an investment bank that handles mergers and acquisitions for energy compa-nies, is the author of Twilight in the Desert: The Coming Saudi Oil Shock and the World Economy. *In the following interview by environmental writer Amanda Griscom Little, Simmons ar-gues that peak oil—when the high-quality, high flow-rate oil has been depleted, and the remaining oil is more difficult and more expensive to recover—is imminent and will cause worldwide economic disruption. His solutions for dealing with the problems caused by slowing production and rapidly increasing world oil use include expanded drilling in Alaska and the Arctic and a movement toward telecommuting.*

As you read, consider the following questions:

1. On what evidence does Simmons base his claim that world peak oil production is near?

2. What was unusual about the author's research on data about world oil production?

3. According to Simmons, what long-term energy solutions must the United States pursue, and how will these change the American way of life?

A manda Griscom Little: *Let's start with a brief overview of the premise and implications of [your book]* Twilight.

Matthew Simmons: I believe we are either at or very close to peak oil. If I'm right, then we have to assume that five or 10 years from now we'll be producing less oil than we are today. And yet we have a society that is expecting, under the most conservative assumptions, that oil usage will grow by at least 30 to 50 percent over the next 25 years. In other words, we would end up with only 70 percent of the oil we have today when we would need to have 150 percent. It's a problem of staggering economic proportions—far greater than the temporary setback of a terrorist attack on energy infrastructure—that could end up leading to more geopolitical fistfights than you can ever imagine. The fistfights turn into weapon fights and give way to a very ugly society.

How did this thesis evolve?

The odyssey began in the early 1980s when I realized that my firm was threatened by a production collapse in the energy and oil-service business. I thought, "How on earth could this have happened without us even knowing?" I started doing some careful investigation into energy data. The more I studied, the more I started to realize that so many people who call themselves experts in the energy market, including government analysts, are in fact experts in their opinions and don't actually base a lot of it in actual data.

Why? Because the relevant data are confidential?

Yes, what's publicly available is extremely vague. No major oil-producing companies or nations allow audits of the data on their reserves and production, which leaves the experts effectively playing a guessing game.

If the data are concealed, on what evidence did you base your own conclusions?

I've spent years poring over hundreds of papers from the Society of Petroleum Engineers that have revealed fascinating clues. First I took an inventory of the top oil fields in the world, field by field. I was aghast to find that nobody had ever listed even the top 20 oil fields by name. I found that there are only about 120 oil fields in the world that produce half of the world's oil supply. The top 14 fields, which make up 20 percent of global supply, are, on average, over 53 years old. In Saudi Arabia, which harbors a quarter of the entire global supply, there are only five key fields producing 90 percent of their oil. They're all old.

Naturally I was very curious to find details on the condition and productivity of these fields. [In 2003] I took a trip to Saudi Arabia on a government tour for business executives. They plied us with various data points that just didn't add up, even vaguely. I've since found evidence in the engineering papers indicating that the major Saudi fields are seriously at risk of reaching their peak, at which point they will begin to see their output decline.

In this case, would Saudi Arabia's leadership collapse?

I want to steer away from discussing specifics of geopolitics in the Middle East because I really don't want to shift the focus away from the economics. It doesn't ultimately matter who rules Saudi Arabia. They can't change the maturity of their oil fields.

Oil Prices Will Skyrocket

You made a $5,000 bet with conservative New York Times *columnist John Tierney that per-barrel oil prices will be at $200 in 2010. How did you arrive at this number?*

Well, first of all, the $5,000 bet was essentially an effort to be provocative and wake people up to how cheap oil still is. I started [in 2004] saying that we need to prepare ourselves for triple-digit oil prices—and I don't mean $100 per barrel, I mean high triple digits. Will it be by 2010? We don't have any idea. It could be by the winter of 2006.

Oil price will ultimately be set by demand and supply. Current oil prices are ridiculously cheap. People find that hard to believe, particularly now, but consider this: $65 a barrel translates to 10 cents a cup. Ten times cheaper than bottled water. People who think that this is a really high price need to have their heads screwed back on.

You have an enormous amount, professionally, riding on the prediction that peak oil is nigh.

I'm basically betting my entire career.

What evidence did you find of looming production limits?

Let's start with the plummeting rate of discovery of critical oil fields. The French Petroleum Institute did a major study a couple of decades ago about the distribution of oil fields by basin, which lends itself to a chessboard analogy. What happens with phenomenal regularity worldwide is that within about five years of moving into a new area of potential oil reserves, prospectors tend to find the queen first, which is the second-largest; within a handful of years they find the king; and then over the next decade you find the next eight to 10 lords. And once you've found the royal family, the rest of the hydrocarbon deposits you'll ever find are basically peons in size. Research overwhelmingly shows that all the royal families have been discovered.

Cartoon by Chuck Asay. Copyright © 2005 Creators Syndicate. By permission of Chuck Asay and Creators Syndicate, Inc.

Can you describe your findings that most of the king- and queen-sized deposits are so old that they have to be injected with increasing amounts of water to produce the crude?

For decades, Saudi Arabia has been injecting water in each key oil field to keep reservoir pressure artificially high. The data show that Saudis are now injecting somewhere between 15 million and 18 million barrels a day of water to recover 8 million barrels a day of oil. This is not sustainable. Geologically speaking, the faster you produce a highly pressurized reservoir, the faster the reservoir pressure collapses. Conversely, the more gently you produce the field, the longer you can produce it at a steady rate, and the higher amount of oil you get out of the field.

I suppose it's safe to assume we're not poised to go gently into the twilight of global reserves.

To put it mildly. What they are doing is rapidly depleting the high-quality, high flow-rate oil, so they'll be left with vast amounts of oil that just won't come out of the ground without massive water input or thousands and thousands of wells being drilled.

What kind of response have you gotten to this book? I saw in a New York Times Magazine *article by Peter Maass that Sadad al-Hussein, a former executive of state-owned Saudi Aramco, essentially corroborated your thesis.*

Yes, he's a first-rate person. We've actually become quite good friends. I don't know to what extent I might have actually liberated him to speak more openly about the limits to Middle East oil. I think I've given quite a few Saudi insiders cover for being able to finally speak up and say, yes, that's actually what I thought, too.

In the U.S., the response within industry and among politicians has been overwhelmingly positive. About 10 people total have attacked the book, and my guess is that most of them have one commonality: a consulting client called Saudi Aramco.

It boggles my mind that data on oil reserves can be concealed. Knowing when we're going to run out would seem as critical to global security as knowing who has weapons of mass destruction [WMDs]. Why isn't disclosing oil data a responsibility on par with disclosing WMDs?

It should be. The foreign minister of Saudi Arabia spoke at Rice University [in Houston, Texas, in September 2005] and he said, "We're as transparent as anybody." And he's right. Until we force that same standard of disclosure on [Western oil giants] Exxon and Shell and BP, then I don't think there's any reason to expect Saudi Arabia to behave better. What I'm suggesting is the whole world needs to go to a new standard. The problem, of course, is this: In political and corporate worlds there are currently significant disincentives to be forthright about these risks. That's why we're going to have to have some sort of enforced mandate. It won't happen voluntarily.

What would you advise the [George W.] Bush administration to do?

Clamor for energy-data reform. That's the only thing the governments of the world can do [in 2005]. But they can't do it alone. I think the global mandate of how we have to attack this problem needs to be a very coordinated, central plan. We need to have international energy cooperation so we don't go into an accidental energy war.

Have you discussed these ideas with President Bush?

I have met with the president quite a few times on energy, but not since coming to these latest conclusions. But I have spoken very openly with senior politicians from both parties, and key people are paying attention.

I understand you are a strong proponent of allowing drilling in the Arctic National Wildlife Refuge and the outer continental shelf.

Yes, ASAP. There's nothing we can do to solve our problems, but everything we do that helps is a bridge to buy us time. Ultimately, we have to actually create some new forms of energy that don't exist today. Solar and wind are, of course, electricity, so not helpful near-term on the transportation front, which is the most intractable part of the problem. Biofuels need to be intensely examined, but corn-based ethanol is a scam because it requires such intensive oil inputs.

What about the shift to hybrid engines and, ultimately, hydrogen?

There are some 220 million cars currently on the road in the U.S. alone. The problem with that concept, which so many people think is the way you end the energy war, is it will take 30 years to turn over the entire vehicle fleet. We don't have 15 or 20 years, much less 30.

We need to think on a grander scale. We have to find, for instance, far more energy-efficient methods of transporting products by rail and ship rather than trucks. We have to liberate the workforce from office-based jobs and let them work in their village, through the modern technology of emails and faxes and video conferencing. We have to address the distribution of food: Much of the food in supermarkets today comes from at least a continent or two away. We need to return to local farms. And we have to attack globalization: As energy prices soar, manufacturing things close to home will begin to make sense again.

| "There will be a large, unprecedented buildup of oil supply in the next few years."

The World Is Not Running Out of Oil

Daniel Yergin

Daniel Yergin is chairman of the energy consulting firm Cambridge Energy Research Associates and the Pulitzer Prize–winning author of The Prize: The Epic Quest for Oil, Money, and Power. *In the following article, Yergin argues that fears of imminent oil shortages are not justified, based on his own analysis of worldwide production capacity. He and his colleagues predict that oil production will increase by 20 percent by 2010, relieving fears that oil shortages are imminent. He also puts current alarm over oil depletion in historical perspective: Cyclic periods of shortages and surplus, he maintains, are normal and have occurred at least five times in the history of the oil industry.*

As you read, consider the following questions:

1. Why does Yergin contend that the specter of an energy shortage is not limited to oil?

2. According to the author, how would new technology be a better predictor of oil capacity and rates of oil production than the current Securities and Exchange Commission formulas used by investors?

3. According to Yergin, what are the long-term challenges for dealing with energy shortages?

We're not running out of oil. Not yet.

"Shortage" is certainly in the air—and in the price. Right now the oil market is tight, even tighter than it was on the eve of the 1973 oil crisis. In this high-risk market, "surprises" ranging from political instability to hurricanes could send oil prices spiking higher. Moreover, the specter of an energy shortage is not limited to oil. Natural gas supplies are not keeping pace with growing demand. Even supplies of coal, which generates about half of the country's electricity, are constrained when our electric power system [is] tested by an extraordinary heat wave.

But it is oil that gets most of the attention. Prices around $60 a barrel, driven by high demand growth, are fueling the fear of imminent shortage—that the world is going to begin running out of oil in five or 10 years. This shortage, it is argued, will be amplified by the substantial and growing demand from two giants: China and India.

Yet this fear is not borne out by the fundamentals of supply. Our new, field-by-field analysis of production capacity, led by my colleagues Peter Jackson and Robert Esser, is quite at odds with the current view and leads to a strikingly different conclusion: There will be a large, unprecedented buildup of oil supply in the next few years. Between 2004 and 2010, capacity to produce oil (not actual production) could grow by 16 million barrels a day—from 85 million barrels per day to 101 million barrels a day—a 20 percent increase. Such growth

Trillions of Barrels of Oil Remain

Saudi Arabia, the biggest oil producer, and Exxon Mobil, the largest oil company [on September 27, 2005], declared that the world had decades' worth of oil to come. . . .

Forming a powerful alliance, the Saudi oil minister Ali al-Naimi said, at an industry conference in Johannesburg, [South Africa], that the country would soon almost double its "proven" reserve base, while Exxon's president, Rex Tillerson, spoke of 3 trillion or more barrels of oil that are yet to be recovered. . . .

Mr. Naimi said talk of oil scarcity reminded him of the 1970s, when people also thought the end of the age of oil was at hand. "But in the intervening years, when we were supposedly facing a precipitous decline, world oil reserves more than doubled," he said.

Saeed Shah, Independent *(UK), September 28, 2005.*

over the next few years would relieve the current pressure on supply and demand.

Where will this growth come from? It is pretty evenly divided between non-OPEC and OPEC [Organization of Petroleum-Exporting Countries]. The largest non-OPEC growth is projected for Canada, Kazakhstan, Brazil, Azerbaijan, Angola and Russia. In the OPEC countries, significant growth is expected to occur in Saudi Arabia, Nigeria, Algeria and Libya, among others. Our estimate for growth in Iraq is quite modest—only 1 million barrels a day—reflecting the high degree of uncertainty there. In the forecast, the United States remains almost level, with development in the deepwater areas of the Gulf of Mexico compensating for declines elsewhere.

While questions can be raised about specific countries, this forecast is not speculative. It is based on what is already unfolding. The oil industry is governed by a "law of long lead times." Much of the new capacity that will become available between now and 2010 is under development. Many of the projects that embody this new capacity were approved in the 2001–03 period, based on price expectations much lower than current prices.

There are risks to any forecast. In this case, the risks are not the "below ground" ones of geology or lack of resources. Rather, they are "above ground"—political instability, outright conflict, terrorism or slowdowns in decision making on the part of governments in oil-producing countries. Yet, even with the scaling back of the forecast, it would still constitute a big increase in output.

Cyclic Shortages and Surpluses Are Normal

This is not the first time that the world has "run out of oil." It's more like the fifth. Cycles of shortage and surplus characterize the entire history of the oil industry. A similar fear of shortage after World War I was one of the main drivers for cobbling together the three easternmost provinces of the defunct Ottoman Turkish Empire to create Iraq. In more recent times, the "permanent oil shortage" of the 1970s gave way to the glut and price collapse of the 1980s.

But this time, it is said, is "different." A common pattern in the shortage periods is to underestimate the impact of technology. And, once again, technology is key. "Proven reserves" are not necessarily a good guide to the future. The current Securities and Exchange Commission disclosure rules, which define "reserves" for investors, are based on 30-year-old technology and offer an incomplete picture of future potential. As skills improve, output from many producing regions will be much greater than anticipated. The share of "unconventional oil"—Canadian oil sands, ultra-deep-water develop-

The Oil Age Is Over

An oil-based economy such as ours doesn't need to deplete its entire reserve of oil before it begins to collapse. A shortfall between demand and supply as little as 10–15 percent is enough to wholly shatter an oil-dependent economy and reduce its citizenry to poverty.

Matthew David Savinar, The Oil Age Is Over, *2004.*

different methods, but their answers have been remarkably similar. The worldwide Hubbert peak, they say, will occur very soon—most probably within this decade [2000–2010]. There are highly respected geologists who disagree with that assessment, and the data on which it is based are subject to dispute. Nevertheless, Hubbert's followers have succeeded in making a crucial point: The worldwide supply of oil, as of any mineral resource, will rise from zero to a peak and after that will decline forever.

Forty More Years?

Some say that the world has enough oil to last for another forty years or more, but that view is almost surely mistaken. The peak, which will occur when we've used half the oil nature made for us, will come far sooner than that. When the peak occurs, increasing demand will meet decreasing supply, possibly with disastrous results. We had a foretaste of the consequences in 1973, when some Middle Eastern nations took advantage of declining U.S. supplies and created a temporary, artificial shortage. The immediate result was long lines at the gas stations, accompanied by panic and despair for the future of the American way of life. After the worldwide Hubbert's peak, the shortage will not be artificial and it will not be temporary.

There are those who see a silver lining in this dire situation. Since the beginning of the Industrial Revolution, we have been pouring carbon dioxide and other greenhouse gases into the atmosphere precisely because of the burning of fossil fuels. Scientists are fairly certain that the result has been an increase in global temperature, and that this will continue and might accelerate. Could it be that Hubbert's peak will save us from destroying our planet?

Earth's Fragile Climate

The climate of Earth is in a fragile, metastable state that was probably created by life itself. Primitive life forms were responsible for oxygenating the atmosphere, and they were also responsible for laying down huge quantities of carbon, in the form of coal and other fossil fuels. If, after Hubbert's peak, we take to burning coal in large quantities, then Earth's so-called intelligent life will be reconverting that carbon and oxygen into carbon dioxide. We cannot predict exactly what that will do to our climate, but one possibility is that it will throw the planet into an entirely different state. The planet Venus is in such a state: Because of a runaway greenhouse effect, its surface temperature is hot enough to melt lead.

The Effects of an Oil Shortage Can Be Drastic

Some economists say that we don't need to worry about running out of oil, because while it's happening the rise in oil prices will make other fuels economically competitive and oil will be replaced by something else. But as we learned in 1973, the effects of an oil shortage can be immediate and drastic, while it may take years, perhaps decades, to replace the vast infrastructure that supports the manufacture, distribution, and consumption of the products of the twenty million barrels of oil we Americans alone gobble up each day.

One certain effect will be steep inflation, because gasoline, along with everything made from petrochemicals and everything that has to be transported, will suddenly cost more. Such an inflationary episode will surely cause severe economic damage—perhaps so severe that we will be unable to replace the world's vast oil infrastructure with something else. That's a prospect we would rather not think about.

Nuclear power plants are so feared and controversial that none have been built in the United States for many years, and some countries (for example, Italy) have outlawed them completely. When the oil crisis comes, opposition to nuclear power is likely to weaken considerably. But it will take at best a decade or more for the first new power plants to come on line—and the use of nuclear fuel is pretty much limited to power plants. Nuclear energy will not easily substitute for oil. Even if we do manage a successful switch to coal or natural gas, we will, in a few reckless generations, have depleted Earth's endowment to us and altered its climate to an extent that we cannot now predict. The only alternative to that dark vision of the future is to learn to live entirely on nuclear power and light as it arrives from the Sun. Will we have the wisdom and ability to do that? If we do, can a civilization as complex as ours live on those resources?

These are big questions, and their answers depend heavily on social and political factors. But there is also a large component of science underlying all of this. We can hope, if we are wise, to alter the laws of peoples. But we cannot change the laws of nature. Those who are not specialists need to learn about both the opportunities and the limitations that nature has provided for us. Only if we understand both can we hope to proceed with wisdom.

> *"Of the alternative fuels and gadgets that are technically viable today, many simply cannot compete with fossil fuels or existing technologies."*

A Transition to Renewable Energy Sources Is Not Feasible

Paul Roberts

The energy alternatives touted as replacements for fossil fuels are all plagued with problems that make their implementation infeasible, according to writer Paul Roberts. Americans expect energy miracles, Roberts says, but are in for a big shock—despite the drawbacks of fossil fuels, no other energy source can compete with petroleum, gas, or coal in terms of cost or performance. Moreover, he warns, the difficulties of dismantling the existing petroleum infrastructure are incalculable, and consumers will opt for "cheap" fossil fuels as long as the market allows. Paul Roberts writes on environmental and economic issues for Harper's Magazine *and is the author of the book* The End of Oil.

As you read, consider the following questions:

1. According to Roberts, what are the pros and cons of relying on natural gas as a "bridge" fuel until viable replacements for oil and coal arrive?

Paul Roberts, "Over a Barrel," *Mother Jones*, November-December 2004. Copyright 2004 Foundation for National Progress. Reproduced by permission.

2. What does the author mean when he describes coal and wind as a "power density mismatch"?

3. Why do hydrogen fuel cells compare unfavorably to fossil fuels, according to the author?

As encouraging as all this new energy awareness is, actually weaning the United States from fossil fuels is far easier said than done. To begin with, our current energy infrastructure—the pipelines and refineries, the power plants and grids, the gasoline stations, and, of course, the cars, trucks, planes, and ships—is a massive, sprawling asset that took more than a century to build and is worth some $1 trillion. Replacing that hydrocarbon monster with "clean" technologies and fuels before our current energy problems escalate into catastrophes will likely be the most complex and expensive challenge this country has ever faced.

And just as we've tended to underplay the flaws in our hydrocarbon energy system, we've also held far too rosy a notion of the various energy alternatives that are supposed to replace oil. In fact, to the extent that most politicians even discuss alternative energy, it tends to be in the rhetoric of American Can-Doism, a triumphant vision in which the same blend of technological prowess, entrepreneurial spirit, and market forces that helped us build an atom bomb, put a man on the moon, and produce the TV dinner and the microchip can now be counted on to yield a similar miracle in energy. Thus we find ourselves imagining a future powered by solar cells, bio-diesel, wind farms, tidal power, cold fusion, and, of course, hydrogen fuel cells, all currently being created in busy research labs and brought to us by a Free Market that is responding naturally, efficiently, and inexorably to the rising price of oil.

Yet the hard truth is that this hyper-optimistic dream is plagued by a variety of potentially killer flaws. First, many of these new technologies are nowhere near ready for prime time and exist mainly in the conceptual stage, if that. Second, of the alternative fuels and gadgets that are technically viable today, many simply cannot compete with fossil fuels or existing technologies. Third, while the market is indeed a marvelous mechanism for bringing innovation to life, the modern economy doesn't even recognize that the current energy system needs replacing. You and I may know that hydrocarbons cost us dearly, in terms of smog, climate change, corruption, and instability, not to mention the billions spent defending the Middle East. But because these "external" costs aren't included in the price of a gallon of gasoline, the market sees no reason to find something other than oil, gas, or coal.

Limitations of Hydrogen and Natural Gas

In late July 2004, financial analysts from across North America joined a conference call with Dennis Campbell, the embattled president of a shrinking Canadian company called Ballard Power Systems. Just a few years before, Ballard had been the toast of energy investors and the acknowledged leader in the campaign to move beyond oil. Its main product, a compact hydrogen fuel cell that could power a car, was widely hailed as the breakthrough that would smash the century-long reign of the gasoline-powered internal combustion engine. In early 2000, Ballard shares were trading for $120, allowing the company to raise a near-record $340.7 million in financing and touching off a wave of expectations that a fuel-cell revolution was imminent.

Since then, however, as fuel cells have been hobbled by technical problems, Ballard has seen its share value plummet to $8, as energy investors have all but abandoned hydrogen in favor of the latest energy darling, the gas-electric hybrid. During the conference call, Campbell insisted that hybrids were only a temporary fix, and that fuel cells remained the only long-term solution to problems like climate change and declining energy supplies. He was, however, forced to acknowledge that consumers and businesses alike were "discouraged by the long wait and the uncertain timelines" for fuel cells and had been "seduced by the lure of an easier solution to the energy and environmental challenges that we face."

In many respects, Ballard is the perfect cautionary tale for the entire roster of alternative fuels and energy technologies, which, for all their huge promise, are, upon closer inspection, plagued by problems. For example, many energy experts see natural gas as the most logical interim step in eventually weaning ourselves from oil. Natural gas emits less carbon dioxide and pollutants than does oil (and certainly coal); it can be used in everything from cars to power plants; it's also easily refined into hydrogen—all of which make it the perfect "bridge" fuel between the current oil-based economy and something new. But even as demand for gas grows in the United States, domestic production is in decline, meaning we'll have to import an increasing volume via pipelines from Canada or through liquefied natural gas terminals in port cities. Even assuming we overcome the political hurdles, simply building this costly new infrastructure will take years, and, once completed, will leave us dependent on many of the same countries that now control the oil business. (The biggest gas reserves are in the Middle East and Russia.)

Above all, gas doesn't solve the climate problem; it merely slows the rate at which we emit carbon dioxide [CO_2]. According to the United Nations Intergovernmental Panel on Climate Change, in order to cut CO_2 emissions fast enough to actually prevent catastrophic warming, we eventually need to produce most of our energy with carbon-free technology. And we're a long way from "most." Today, hydrocarbons own the energy market—40 percent of our energy comes from oil, 23 percent each from gas and coal. Nuclear provides around 8 percent, while renewable, carbon-free energy accounts for barely 5 percent of our total energy supply. Of that "good" energy, nearly 90 percent comes from hydroelectric dams, which are so expensive and environmentally nasty that their future

Alternative Pipe Dreams

The widely touted "hydrogen economy" is a particularly cruel hoax. We are not going to replace the U.S. automobile and truck fleet with vehicles that run on fuel cells. For one thing, the current generation of fuel cells is largely designed to run on hydrogen obtained from natural gas. The other way to get hydrogen in the quantities wished for would be electrolysis of water using power from hundreds of nuclear plants. Apart from the dim prospect of our building that many nuclear plants soon enough, there are also numerous severe problems with hydrogen's nature as an element that present forbidding obstacles to its use as a replacement for oil and gas, especially in storage and transport.

James Howard Kunstler, Rolling Stone, *April 13, 2005.*

role is extremely limited. The rest comes mainly from "biomass" usually plants and crop waste that are either refined into fuels, like ethanol, or burned to make steam.

Limitations of Solar and Wind

And what about solar and wind? As it turns out, the two most famous alternative energy technologies together generate less than half a percent of the planet's energy. Here's a depressing fact: The entire output of every solar photovoltaic (PV) cell currently installed worldwide—about 2,000 megawatts total—is less than the output of just two conventional, coal-fired power plants.

Why do alternatives own such a puny share of the market? According to conventional wisdom, Big Oil and Big Coal use their massive economic power to corrupt Big Government, which then hands out massive subsidies and tax breaks for oil and coal, giving hydrocarbons an unbeatable advantage over alternatives. In truth, much of the fault lies with the new energy technologies themselves, which simply cannot yet compete effectively with fossil fuels.

Consider the saga of the solar cell. Despite decades of research and development, solar power still costs more than electricity generated from a gas- or coal-fired power plant. And although PV cell costs will continue to fall, there remains the problem of "intermittency"—solar only works when the sun is shining, whereas a conventional power plant can crank out power 24 hours a day, 365 days a year. (Wind presents a similar problem.) To use solar and wind, utilities must have backup power, probably coal- or gas-fired plants.

Eventually, utilities will solve the intermittency problem—probably with superfast "smart" power grids that can connect wind or solar farms built across the nation, or even the hemisphere, effectively getting power from wherever the sun is shining or the wind is blowing and delivering it to customers. But the very scale of this solution illustrates an even more serious weakness for wind and other renewables: They lack the "power density" of the fossil fuels they seek to replace. Coal, for example, packs a great deal of stored energy in a relatively small volume. As a result, a coal-fired plant requires only a few hundred acres of space, yet can supply electricity for 200,000 homes. By contrast, to generate equal power from wind, which is far less power-dense, you'd need a wind farm of more than 200 square miles in size. Given that by 2030, almost 60 percent of the global population is expected to live in cities of 1 million or more, meeting our power needs with wind, solar, or other renewables will be challenging indeed. "Supplying those buildings from locally generated renewable energies is either impractical or impossible," says Vaclav Smil, an expert in energy economies at the University of Manitoba. The "power-density mismatch is simply too large."

The most dramatic example of the mismatch between fossil fuels and their would-be competitors, however, can be found in the fuel cell. For decades, hydrogen proponents have argued that fuel cells, which turn hydrogen and oxygen into electricity while emitting only water vapor, are the key to the next energy economy. Like a battery that never needs charging, fuel cells can power office buildings, laptops, and especially cars, where they are roughly three times as efficient as a traditional internal combustion engine. And because you can make hydrogen by running electric current through water, advocates envisioned a global system in which power from solar, wind, and other renewables would be turned into hydrogen.

This compelling vision helps explain why the "hydrogen economy" was so touted during the 1990s, and why companies like Ballard Power Systems could partner with giants like DaimlerChrysler and Ford, igniting a fuel-cell mania that dazzled investors and policymakers alike. Indeed, in his 2003 State of the Union address, President [George W.] Bush vowed that, within 20 years, fuel cells would "make our air significantly cleaner, and our country much less dependent on foreign sources of oil."

In truth, even as the president was promising better living through hydrogen, the reality of a hydrogen economy was moving farther and farther away. While the basic technology remains promising, making hydrogen turns out to be far more difficult than advertised. The easiest and by far cheapest method—splitting natural gas into carbon and hydrogen—is hampered by domestic shortages of natural gas. And while it is possible to extract hydrogen from water using renewably generated electricity, that concept suffers from the power-density problem. Studies by Jim MacKenzie, a veteran energy analyst with the World Resources Institute, show that a solar-powered hydrogen economy in the United States would require at least 160,000 square miles of photovoltaic panels—an area slightly larger than the state of California—and would increase national water consumption by 10 percent. "We could do it," MacKenzie told me [in 2003]. "But it would be expensive."

But hydrogen's biggest problem is the fuel cell itself, which, despite decades of research, is still too expensive and unreliable to compete with the internal combustion engine. As of [2003], the best fuel cells were still 10 times as costly as an equivalently powered gasoline engine. Hydrogen advocates argue that once fuel cells can be mass-produced, costs will drop dramatically. Yet while that's true, it's also true that gasoline engines will also improve over time—in fact, they already have. With the gasoline-electric hybrid, for example, the internal combustion engine has, in a stroke, doubled its fuel economy and halved its emissions—but without forcing consumers to use a complicated new technology or fuel. Barring some technological breakthrough that dramatically lowers costs or improves performance, the fuel cell may remain one step behind the gasoline engine for a long time, further delaying the moment it can begin displacing its hydrocarbon rival.

Constraints of the Market Economy

This, then, is the central dilemma facing the architects of the next energy economy. Left to themselves, markets will indeed move us to new energy technologies, but these technologies may not be the ones we ultimately want or need. For example, while the hybrid does cut emissions and fuel use, as Ballard's Campbell testily points out, hybrids "still require fossil fuel" and thus can only be an interim solution. To be sure, interim solutions are essential, but if we concentrate only on half-measures, long-term technologies may not become economically viable fast enough to stave off an implosion of our energy system—be it from runaway climate change in 2015 or the collapse of the Saudi government in 2005.

Thus a true energy revolution—one that begins moving away from fossil fuels entirely—can't succeed or even get started until we can somehow induce the market to "see" the true costs of energy, and, specifically, just how environmentally and politically expensive "cheap" fossil fuels really are.

> "Many of America's security and eco-
> nomic problems stem from its depen-
> dence on oil imported from unstable
> parts of the world."

Alternative Energy Sources Are Necessary to Reduce U.S. Dependence on Foreign Oil

Institute for the Analysis of Global Security

*U.S. national security is seriously threatened by the country's de-
pendence on imported oil, according to the Institute for the
Analysis of Global Security (IAGS), a nonprofit public educational organization based in Washington, D.C. In the following
article, the IAGS describes the initiative Set America Free,
adopted in 2004 by a group of national policy experts to waken
Americans to the military and economic costs of buying oil from
countries that fund anti-American terrorism. The author maintains that the sooner the United States can develop and implement energy technologies based on existing infrastructure, such
as hybrid vehicles, and abundant domestic energy sources, such
as coal and electricity, the safer Americans will be.*

As you read, consider the following questions:

1. According to Milton Copulos of the National Defense Council Foundation, how much does America's dependence on foreign oil cost in military-budget dollars and lost jobs?

2. Why would shifting electrical power generation to sources other than oil fail to reduce America's dependence on foreign oil, according to IAGS planner Anne Korin?

3. What resources does the Set America Free initiative endorse in place of imported oil?

On September 27, 2004 a group of national security experts and representatives of prominent Washington think tanks and public policy organizations, including the Institute for the Analysis of Global Security (IAGS), Foundation for Defense of Democracies (FDD,) Center for Security Policy, Hudson Institute, National Defense Council Foundation (NDCF), and the American Council on Renewable Energy (ACORE,) released an open letter to Americans and an accompanying blueprint for energy security called "Set America Free," calling for immediate action toward reduction of America's demand for oil. The document spells out practical steps which can be undertaken over the [years 2005–2009] and beyond to dramatically improve America's energy security. Members of the group called upon America's leaders to adopt the plan, with a view to rapidly expanding fuel choice in the U.S. transportation sector beyond petroleum while exploiting currently available technologies and infrastructures. If the plan is carried out in full, U.S. oil imports would drop by as much as 50 percent.

While until recently the alternative fuel message had been the territory of environmentalists, this changed September 11 [2001], when it became evident that many of America's security and economic problems stem from its dependence on oil imported from unstable parts of the world. In fact, the U.S. is facing today a "perfect storm" of strategic, energy, economic and environmental conditions that demand a dramatic reduction in the quantities of imported oil. Dealing with the problem will no doubt be a daunting task. . . .

"Set America Free began with the proposition that we have a serious security problem and we need to look at existing vehicle types and processes to make transportation fuels that can run in these vehicles. And we need to do it now," said James Woolsey, one of the effort's leaders. Gal Luft, executive director of IAGS, noted that America's relations with countries that own most of the world's oil reserves are at an all time low. "If you look at every global conflict we have faced in the past, there was always a technological component. We always had technology as a game changer. And this conflict calls for one as well."

Frank Gaffney, president of the Center for Security Policy, said: "We are funding terrorism with our petrodollars. The bulk of the funding for terrorism is money that flows from state sponsors of terrorism and from there to terrorist organizations. In other words we're paying them to kill us. . . . As one who approaches this from a pure national security perspective I really believe we have no choice but to seize the opportunity to move the country as rapidly as possible off the vulnerability associated with this current reliance on foreign oil." He called for the next president to take active measures to reduce America's oil dependence. "With the right leadership the effects of the plan can begin to be felt within the next four years." Milton Copulos, who heads the NDCF, made a strong economic rationale for adopting the $12 billion plan. He described the economic costs associated with gasoline, many of which do not show up at the gas station: "We spend $49 billion every year to maintain the capability to intervene militarily in the Persian Gulf. The U.S. is also losing 828,000 jobs every year due to its dependence on foreign oil." Copulos

Foreign Oil Makes America Vulnerable to Terrorism

The bottom line: The greater our dependence on foreign oil, the greater our exposure to the will of other nations and terrorists. World events in 2004, including violence in Iraq, terrorist attacks in Saudi Arabia, and political maneuvering in Russia, all strongly affected the price of oil and, more important, demonstrate the vulnerability of the United States. As oil demand in North America and China continues to climb, we must assess the future stability of the U.S. oil supply.

Richard A. Clarke et al., "Defeating the Jihadists,"
The Century Foundation, November 16, 2004.

said that the U.S. is losing $305 billion every year as a result of its dependence. "Isn't it worth it to spend one percent of what we spend to subsidize our enemies to create almost a million jobs at home and finally free ourselves from the dangers of our oil supply vulnerabilities?"

Anne Korin, director of policy and strategic planning at IAGS, explained that the Set America Free project analyzed the costs and benefits, time frame for commercialization, feasibility, and economic impact of each path to energy security. "We worked with energy, technology, and policy experts with a wide variety of expertise to develop a plan that could significantly reduce our dependence on oil within a reasonable time frame and at reasonable cost. . . . Since two-thirds of our oil is consumed in the transportation sector, displacing oil in this sector was our focus. Only 2% of electricity in the U.S. is generated from oil so shifting power generation away from oil does not solve our problem. Additionally, we realize that full market transformation of the transportation sector is a very long process—15 to 20 years. That is exactly why we must start this process without delay."

Use Existing Infrastructure and Domestic Resources

Set America Free upholds a number of principles: Due to the urgency of the issue, the coalition believes that there is no time to wait for the commercialization of technologies that are still at the research and development phase. The group believes the U.S. should implement technologies that are ready for deployment and simply need a push to enter the mass market. Bill Holmberg of ACORE, a member of the coalition, remarked that it makes more sense to use electricity to power plug-in hybrid vehicles (PHEV), a technology that exists today, than to use it to produce hydrogen to fuel vehicles in a technology that is still far in the future.

The coalition also believes that rather than investing significant time and resources in developing new refueling and distribution infrastructure it makes most sense to rely on existing infrastructure to the extent possible. The coalition emphasized that the U.S. should better utilize its domestic energy resources. While America is not rich in oil nor in natural gas, it has a wealth of other energy sources, among them a quarter of the world's coal supply, abundant biomass, municipal waste, and electricity sources such as nuclear power plants, solar, wind, hydro and geothermal power. All of these resources can be used to produce made-in-America transportation fuels that are not made from petroleum.

While the group's prime concern is national security, its members recognize the need to be sensitive to environmental concerns, and they encourage green groups to join the coalition. All the solutions proposed are far more environmentally friendly than the status quo.

The coalition called upon the American public and its representatives and shapers of public opinion to endorse the Set

America Free plan and put energy security at the top of the national agenda. The Natural Resources Defense Council (NRDC) has already responded to the call. "This is an effort to bring together tree huggers, do gooders, sod busters and cheap hawks to agree on a common approach," said James Woolsey. "It's a very good coalition."

"*The words 'energy independence' are potentially disastrous ones.*"

Replacing Foreign Oil Imports with Alternatives Would Be Disastrous

Justin Fox

In the following article, journalist Justin Fox warns that a rush to cut supplies of imported oil would have disastrous consequences for the United States. Fox argues, for example, that making imported oil prohibitively expensive would only make fuel prices and unemployment skyrocket and quickly deplete domestic oil reserves, decreasing rather than increasing national security. The most sensible energy strategy, he maintains, is to use the cheapest sources possible, and that means continuing to buy Mideast oil. Justin Fox is the editor-at-large for Fortune *magazine.*

As you read, consider the following questions:

1. According to Fox, what simple step would immediately achieve energy independence, if that is really what Americans want?

2. As cited by Fox, what does economist Austan Goolsbee argue would be the actual undesirable effect of conserving oil?

3. According to the author, what optimal per-gallon gas tax would be a more cost-effective way of addressing global warming than cutting oil imports?

It may be one of the most dangerous phrases in the English language. It certainly is one of the most expensive.

I speak of "energy independence," a rallying cry since the oil crisis of the 1970s and one that has been getting a ton of ink (and pixels) lately, especially since President [George W.] Bush brought up the subject in his [2006] State of the Union address.

The president didn't actually utter those words, saying instead that he wanted to "make our dependence on Middle Eastern oil a thing of the past." But lots of other people have, most notably Tom Friedman of *The New York Times*, who has been arguing for a while now that the president should make energy independence our generation's Sputnik[1]—an excuse to spend tons of money on scientific research and education.

Investing in R&D [research and development] and handing out scholarships for science and engineering students are good things, mind you, and many of those calling for energy independence are driven by similarly wholesome motives. But I'm a big believer that words count, and the words "energy independence" are potentially disastrous ones.

To put it most starkly: We could have energy independence tomorrow if Congress simply slapped a huge tariff on energy imports (would $250 per barrel of oil do it?). Meanwhile, skyrocketing fuel prices would shift the economy into reverse, throw tens of millions of Americans out of work, and

1. The Soviet Union launched the first earth-orbiting satellite, Sputnik I, in 1957, which set off the so-called space race between the United States and the Soviet Union, each trying to be the first nation to put a man on the moon. The U.S. space program became a budget priority during that time.

Energy Independence Is Impossible

The United States will always rely on foreign imports of oil to feed its energy needs and should stop trying to become energy independent, a top Exxon Mobil Corp. executive said [in February 2006].

"Realistically, it is simply not feasible in any time period relevant to our discussion today," Exxon Mobil Senior Vice President Stuart McGill said, referring to what he called the "misperception" that the United States can achieve energy independence. . . .

Many in the United States believe America should wean itself off oil imports from the Middle East, fearing it makes the country dangerously dependent on an unstable region.

The world's largest publicly traded oil company, however, says hoping to end foreign oil imports is not only a bad idea, but also impossible.

"Americans depend upon imports to fill the gap," McGill said. "No combination of conservation measures, alternative energy sources and technological advances could realistically and economically provide a way to completely replace those imports in the short or medium term."

Instead of trying to achieve energy independence, importing nations like the U.S. should be promoting energy interdependence, McGill said.

"Because we are all contributing to and drawing from the same pool of oil, all nations—exporting and importing—are inextricably bound to one another in the energy marketplace."

Reuters, "Exxon: America Will Always Rely on Foreign Oil,"
February 7, 2006.

what oil and natural gas we have left under our territory would be rapidly depleted.

Yes, homegrown energy alternatives like wind, solar and ethanol would get a big boost. But the biggest boom would probably be in mining and burning coal—the dirtiest and least efficient of the fossil fuels, but one the United States possesses in abundance. Meanwhile, the other energy-importing countries of the world would go their merry way, paying vastly lower prices for oil and natural gas and gaining a huge competitive advantage as a result.

Nobody's seriously proposing such drastic action, of course. But the scenario above ought to make clear that energy independence isn't really what we want. What we want is the most possible economic bang for our energy buck, plus freedom from the feeling that a handful of oil exporting countries hold our national interest in their hands.

It also would be nice if our energy sources polluted as little as possible—although you can include that under getting economic bang for the buck, since pollution clearly has a long-run economic cost.

Why Sentence Ourselves to More Expensive Energy?

The simplest way to get the most out of what we spend on energy is to keep energy costs cheap, and the best way to do that is to take full advantage of global energy markets. Right now it costs less to pump oil from the sands of the Arabian peninsula than from pretty much anywhere else on earth. Why exactly would we want to punish ourselves by cutting ourselves off from the cheapest oil?

Especially since, as University of Chicago economist Austan Goolsbee pointed out in *Fortune* [magazine] in August [2005], efforts to conserve oil will, by driving prices down, increase our dependence on Middle East oil in particular at the same time that they're decreasing our dependence on oil in general.

Of course, using energy more efficiently is another way to get more economic value out of it. And if we really want to feel less dependent on Middle East oil, we need to develop cost-effective alternatives to oil. This is presumably where the government should come in. But government programs to reduce dependence on foreign oil tend to devolve into boondoggles only a lobbyist could love. . . .

Taxes—on gasoline, or on the carbon-content of fuels if it's global warming you're most concerned about—are a much less messy and market-friendly means of achieving the same goals. By making energy more expensive, of course, they do cut into economic activity.

But there is surely a happy mean: In an article in the September 2005 *American Economic Review* titled "Does Britain or the United States Have the Right Gasoline Tax?" economists Ian Parry and Kenneth Small calculated that the economically optimal gas tax for the U.S. would be about $1.01 a gallon, up from 40 cents now, while for Britain (where roads are more congested, and the economic value of getting people out of their cars is thus greater) it would be $1.34, down from $2.80.

Of course, achieving an economically optimal result doesn't sound nearly as exciting as achieving "energy independence." But it would be a lot less of a pain.

Periodical Bibliography

The following articles have been selected to supplement the diverse views presented in this chapter.

Charli Coon	"Talking Points," Heritage Foundation, 2004. www.issues-2004.org.
James C. Cooper and Kathleen Madigan	"Pricier Oil Won't Send Economy into a Skid," *Business Week*, July 11, 2005.
Robert L. Hirsch, Roger Bezdek, and Robert Wendling	"Mitigating a Long-Term Shortfall of World Oil Production," *WorldOil.com*, May 2005. http://worldoil.com.
Julian Jackson	"How to Deceive Friends and Influence People: Oil Crisis Lies," AxisofLogic.com, March 14, 2005. www.axisoflogic.com.
Daniel Kammen	"Lack of Vision on Policy Clouds Energy Future," *San Francisco Chronicle*, May 13, 2005.
National Wildlife Federation	"On the Hill: Global Warming Proves to Be an Issue in Energy Bill Debate," June 22, 2005. www.nwf.org.
Christopher Palmeri	"Is There Plenty of Oil?" *BusinessWeek*, July 11, 2005.
Fred Pearce	"Squeaky Clean Fossil Fuels," *New Scientist*, May 2, 2005.
Union of Concerned Scientists	"Renewable Energy Can Help Ease Natural Gas Crunch," March 2004. www.ucsusa.org.
Vijay V. Vaitheeswaran	"Consider the Alternatives: Is the Age of Oil Drawing to a Close?" *Economist*, April 28, 2005.
Caspar Weinberger	"A Quest for Energy—a Decades-Long Debate," *Forbes*, June 6, 2005.

CHAPTER 2

Is Nuclear Power a Viable Energy Alternative?

Chapter Preface

On July 16, 1945, the United States detonated the first atomic bomb at a desert test site in New Mexico. Less than a month later the United Stated dropped atomic bombs on the Japanese cities of Hiroshima and Nagasaki, forcing the surrender of Japan and the end of World War II. This military use of atomic power prompted not only a postwar arms race but also an international race to harness nuclear energy for economic purposes.

U.S. president Dwight D. Eisenhower, in a landmark 1953 speech dubbed "Atoms for Peace," hailed nuclear power as a great potential source of domestic energy and decried its destructive potential. Few, however, understood at that time the complexities, difficulties, and costs of building and maintaining nuclear power plants. Controversy has dogged the nuclear power industry ever since.

John Ritch, director general of the World Nuclear Association, and others who support the increased use of nuclear power argue that the continued burning of fossil fuels to generate electricity for growing populations and economies speeds up the global warming process and causes irreparable and devastating damage to the environment. In recent years some environmentalists have joined the movement in support of nuclear power, arguing that the risk of radioactive contamination and the problems of radioactive waste disposal are now outweighed by the immediate dangers of global warming caused by fossil-fuel consumption. Advocates of the construction of up to two thousand new nuclear power plants maintain that nuclear energy is emission free, an already proven technology, and much less expensive to produce than so-called renewable energy sources.

Leading antinuclear activists such as Australian physician Helen Caldicott make a strong case for discontinuing the use of nuclear energy. They argue that every step of the production process for nuclear power, for example, requires fossil fuels and thus produces emissions that potentially contribute to global warming, and point to studies suggesting that radiation from nuclear power plants has increased the incidence of cancer among workers and nearby communities. Harvey Blatt, professor of geology at the Institute of Earth Sciences at Hebrew University of Jerusalem, describes the terrible aftermath of the 1986 nuclear power plant accident at Chernobyl in the Soviet Union as reason enough to discontinue nuclear energy production: Nuclear energy systems, Blatt claims, are inherently dangerous and simply too vulnerable to human error. Antinuclear sentiment has had a significant effect on the industry in the late twentieth century. No new reactors have been built since 1974, and the 103 reactors currently active are all reaching the end of their license: All will have to petition the Nuclear Regulatory Commission (NRC) during the next 20 years to renew their production license, and it is uncertain whether these aging facilities will meet operating standards.

Perry A. Fischer of *World Oil Magazine* defends fossil fuels against supporters of nuclear energy. Fischer argues that the costs of building the plants, safety measures, and fuel are not included in calculations of the price of electricity generated by nuclear power and therefore consumers mistakenly underestimate the real price of nuclear energy. Eric Young of the Union of Concerned Scientists agrees, maintaining that nuclear energy appears cheaper because the U.S. government has been underwriting its costs including the cost of accident insurance.

How to dispose of low- and high-level nuclear waste is another highly controversial issue. Even such low-level waste as contaminated hand tools and shoe covers used at nuclear facilities can contain radioactive elements with a hazardous life of hundreds of thousands of years, and virtually every proposal to store or dispose of nuclear wastes meets with strong opposition from communities near the site or along transit routes. The Yucca Mountain controversy is the prime example of the waste disposal dilemma. The federal government proposes to transport all the country's nuclear wastes by railroad to an underground storage facility near Las Vegas called Yucca Mountain. The state of Nevada, Native American tribes, environmentalists, and many others are suing the federal government in an effort to thwart what they charge is a disastrous plan, charging among other objections that Yucca Mountain is in an earthquake-prone zone and that storage casks are not sufficiently well designed. Opponent Michael Wald contends that Yucca Mountain will never be accepted as a disposal site and suggests that nuclear wastes could be stored in special casks at a central location as an interim effort until future generations can establish a better storage method. Wald and others debate whether nuclear power is a viable alternative to fossil fuels in the following chapter.

> "In the century ahead, nuclear energy
> will be nothing less than indispensable
> if we are to . . . cope with our world's
> vast and expanding human needs."

Nuclear Power Is the Energy of the Future

John Ritch

In the following viewpoint, John Ritch argues that nuclear energy will be an indispensable solution to the looming, global environmental crisis caused by a rapidly growing population and increasing demand for finite fossil fuels. Environmentalists, says Ritch, should discard the fiction that "new renewables" such as solar and wind power can meet human needs. Sustainability, and the urgent need to reduce greenhouse gases, he maintains, requires sharp increases in nuclear energy. John Ritch is director general of the World Nuclear Association (WNA), a global organization whose institutional member companies produce some 90 percent of the nuclear-powered electricity outside the United States.

John Ritch, "A Global Crisis, a Crucial Profession: The Indispensable Role of Nuclear Energy in the 21st Century," speech to the International Youth Nuclear Congress, Toronto, Canada, www.world-nuclear.org, May 20, 2004. Reproduced by permission of the author.

As you read, consider the following questions:

1. What are the environmental challenges facing the world today, according to Ritch?

2. How will nuclear energy help the world deal with the projected levels of greenhouse gases, according to the author?

3. Why does Ritch say that a future in which nuclear power plays a central role will require not radical change but only an acceleration in current trends?

In the century ahead, nuclear energy will be nothing less than indispensable if we are to meet the greatest challenge humankind has ever faced—which is to cope with our world's vast and expanding human needs without destroying the very Earthly environment that enabled our civilization to evolve.

Our planet's fragile biosphere is now at risk, and history has reached a momentous point where the fate of humanity hinges on whether we can summon the will and the ingenuity to produce clean energy on a massive global scale—a scale our nations cannot realistically hope to attain without an expansive use of nuclear power.

To fail in this is to invite real and unmitigated catastrophe—for people everywhere and for our global environment.

Today there are some 440 nuclear power reactors, generating one-sixth of the world's electricity. With global energy demand steadily rising, a clean-energy future will require thousands of reactors—producing not only electricity but also hydrogen and clean water—if we are to mount a concerted strategy to avert environmental catastrophe.

Dimensions of the Global Environmental Crisis

For many environmentalists, any such projection will still seem shocking if not sacrilegious. But if organised environmentalists have not yet embraced nuclear power, they have helped to build awareness of the crisis we truly face:

- They have warned cogently of the enormous consequences—human and environmental—of our world's unprecedented explosion in human numbers.

- They have warned compassionately that, of today's 6 billion people, more than half live in dire conditions— and that we must urgently find new ways to meet these needs without jeopardising the global environment.

- They have warned alarmingly that expanding populations are quickly depleting the world's precious supplies of fresh water, lowering water tables so drastically that, within 25 years, half the world's people could be without reliable access to potable water—unless we can somehow achieve large-scale desalination of water from our oceans and seas.

- They have warned that we face new energy needs in the rising global demand for food and housing and basic services, and they have warned of the dire consequences—through pollution and global warming—if those needs are met by continued use of fossil fuel.

- They have warned that stark evidence of global warming is already all around us: that the hottest years in recorded history have occurred in the past decade, that weather catastrophes are on the rise, and that icecaps and glaciers are melting from Africa to Alaska.

- They have warned that global warming could, within this century, raise sea levels by as much as 20 feet, submerging thousands of islands worldwide, flooding major coastal cities like New York and London, and inundating countries like Bangladesh.

- They have warned that the ongoing melting of the Arctic iceberg and Greenland's huge icesheet could entirely disrupt the Atlantic Gulf Stream, bringing to an end the benign delivery of warm air and water to Western Europe—thereby leaving the British Isles, and even much of continental Europe, with climates as cold and severe as Iceland's is today.

- They have warned that global warming is greatly accelerating the worldwide loss of biodiversity, so much so that, within the next 50 years alone, a full one-fourth of all species on our planet—I repeat, a full one-fourth of all species within the next 50 years—will be lost to extinction, never to appear on Earth again.

This is a powerful message of global crisis. Sceptics, cynics, curmudgeons—and, ironically, many conservatives—may wish to ignore it. For my own part, I find the environmentalist case compelling, profoundly alarming and a clear summons to public action.

The Urgent Necessity of a Decisive Strategic Response

Let us state the case—both the problem and the logic of its solution—in the clearest possible terms: In the next 50 years, as global population grows from 6 to 9 billion, human need will multiply—and, in the absence of dramatic measures, so too will human misery. As nations try to meet this need, the rate of world energy consumption will double or even triple, and—in just this narrow 50-year period alone—humankind will use more energy than in all previous history combined. Today, despite much rhetoric and diplomacy, the global rate of CO_2 [carbon dioxide] emissions—now 25 billion tonnes a year, or 800 tonnes a second—continues to rise inexorably and so too does the atmospheric build-up of these heat-trapping gases.

Stronger Future for Nuclear Power

About 16% of the world's electricity supply comes from nuclear power, and energy demand is increasing. Worldwide, nearly 80% of the 441 commercial nuclear reactors currently in operation are more than 15 years old. To maintain nuclear power's position in the overall energy mix, new reactors will have to replace decommissioned ones.

Paul Guinnessy, Physics Today, *February 2006.*

The implications of this unprecedented accumulation can be found in the Earth's history over the last 400,000 years, which shows CO_2 levels fluctuating between 200 and 300 parts-per-million and atmospheric temperature fluctuating—by about 15 degrees Centigrade—in almost perfect correlation. Now, however, human activity in the industrial age has suddenly—in geological time—raised CO_2 concentrations to well above any pre-industrial level. Today's level of 350 parts-per-million might in itself sound less than alarming. What is undeniably alarming, however, is the projected level. Unless we achieve prompt and drastic global action to curb greenhouse emissions, atmospheric concentrations of CO_2 will reach double the pre-industrial level by the middle of the 21st century and will continue to rise thereafter. To stabilise greenhouse gases—even at a dangerously higher level—scientists calculate that daily global emissions must be cut, within the next 50 years, by at least 50%. Since developing countries such as China and India will inevitably emit far more greenhouse gases, the already industrialised countries must, if we are to preserve the biosphere, cut emissions by 75%—and also lead in disseminating clean-energy technology worldwide.

The Crucial Contribution of Nuclear Energy

We face a future of radical change. Either we will achieve radical transformation in the global economy or we will experience a radical upsurge in human suffering and a radical alteration in the global environment. How are we to accomplish a massive worldwide shift to clean energy technologies? Authoritative projections by the International Energy Agency (in the public sector) and the World Energy Council (in the private sector) point unambiguously to the same conclusion—that our need for clean energy on a colossal scale cannot conceivably be met without a sharply increased use of nuclear power.

In fact, nuclear power is the quintessential sustainable development technology:

Its fuel will be available for multiple centuries, its safety record is superior among major energy sources, its consumption causes virtually no pollution, its use preserves precious fossil resources for future generations, its costs are competitive and declining, and its waste can be securely managed over the long-term. The world's environmentalists have performed many valuable services. But they can provide their fellow citizens no greater service now than to discard the fiction that conservation, solar panels and windmills alone can meet human needs. Sustainability requires nuclear energy; and the path of sound environmentalism today is to embrace, fight for—and finance—a future in which nuclear power and "new renewables" function as clean-energy partners in a transformed global economy.

Achieving consensus on the value of a nuclear-renewables partnership is all the more vital because another atomic marvel—the ability to unite hydrogen and oxygen to make electricity—is about to transform our daily world and lift our prospects for a clean-energy future. Hydrogen offers a means, for the first time in history, to store enormous quantities of electricity—for use, on demand, in cleanly powered transportation and in the full range of traditional electrical uses for home and industry. But hydrogen's environmental value depends on making it cleanly—using the clean primary energy that only nuclear power can provide on a vast scale. Hydrogen provides the bridge by which nuclear power can contribute not just to base-load electricity but to the entire spectrum of energy use. With this bridge, it is now possible for the first time to envisage a thriving, large-scale, emissions-free industrial economy—with nuclear power and renewables providing clean primary energy for direct electricity and for electricity storage via hydrogen.

A future in which nuclear power plays a central role in producing electricity, hydrogen, and clean water will not require a radical change—but only an acceleration—in current trends:

- For four consecutive decades—including the 1990's—nuclear power has been the fastest growing major energy source in the world.

- Today thirty-one nations representing 2/3 of humanity have nuclear power;

- Important nations representing an additional half-billion people—including Indonesia and Vietnam—are planning to use it for the first time;

- Nations representing half of world population are building nuclear power plants, with 30 reactors under construction and 34 more definitely planned;

- The U.S. nuclear industry, owners of the world's largest nuclear fleet, plans 50% growth over the next 20 years; and

- Nuclear planners in the world's largest nations, China and India, envisage at least 250 reactors in each country by mid-century—targets we must hope they will exceed if the biosphere is to be preserved.

The essential issue about nuclear power is not whether it will grow but how fast:

- Will it grow fast enough to meet the world's urgent need for clean energy on a massive scale?

- Will we further strengthen the global infrastructure of people and institutions to guide and promote its growth?

> *"Contrary to the nuclear industry's propaganda, nuclear power is . . . not green and it is certainly not clean."*

Nuclear Energy Is Not the Energy of the Future

Helen Caldicott

According to Australian-born physician and antinuclear activist Helen Caldicott, the nuclear industry is waging a misleading propaganda campaign to portray nuclear power as a panacea for environmental and energy crises. In the following viewpoint, Caldicott contends that nuclear energy is actually not emission-free, not safe, and not fossil-fuel-free. She also maintains that nuclear power plants are vulnerable to terrorist attack, with potentially catastrophic consequences over and above the risks of radioactive waste. Helen Caldicott is founder and president of the Nuclear Policy Research Institute, which opposes the use of nuclear energy and cofounder of Physicians for Social Responsibility.

As you read, consider the following questions:

1. According to Caldicott, how does nuclear power production actually require fossil fuels?

2. What evidence does Caldicott offer that nuclear reactors do produce harmful emissions?

3. What nuclear waste storage problems does the author portray as nuclear energy's "toxic legacy"?

There is a huge propaganda push by the nuclear industry to justify nuclear power as a panacea for the reduction of global-warming gases. . . .

But I would suggest that all the relevant facts be taught to students. Mandatory courses in medical schools should embrace the short- and long-term biological, genetic and medical dangers associated with the nuclear fuel cycle. Business students should examine the true costs associated with the production of nuclear power. Engineering students should become familiar with the profound problems associated with the storage of long-lived radioactive waste, the human fallibilities that have created the most serious nuclear accidents in history and the ongoing history of near-misses and near-meltdowns in the industry.

Nuclear Reactors Are Not Practical

At present there are 442 nuclear reactors in operation around the world. If, as the nuclear industry suggests, nuclear power were to replace fossil fuels on a large scale, it would be necessary to build 2,000 large, 1,000-megawatt reactors. Considering that no new nuclear plant has been ordered in the US since 1978, this proposal is less than practical. Furthermore, even if we decided today to replace all fossil-fuel-generated electricity with nuclear power, there would only be enough economically viable uranium to fuel the reactors for three to four years.

The true economies of the nuclear industry are never fully accounted for. The cost of uranium enrichment is subsidised by the US government. The true cost of the industry's liability in the case of an accident in the US is estimated to be $US560 billion, but the industry pays only $US9.1 billion—98 per cent of the insurance liability is covered by the US federal government. The cost of decommissioning all the existing US nuclear reactors is estimated to be $US33 billion. These costs—plus the enormous expense involved in the storage of radioactive waste for a quarter of a million years—are not now included in the economic assessments of nuclear electricity.

It is said that nuclear power is emission-free. The truth is very different.

In the U.S., where much of the world's uranium is enriched, including Australia's, the enrichment facility at Paducah, Kentucky, requires the electrical output of two 1000-megawatt coal-fired plants, which emit large quantities of carbon dioxide, the gas responsible for 50 per cent of global warming.

Also, this enrichment facility and another at Portsmouth, Ohio, release from leaky pipes 93 per cent of the chlorofluorocarbon [CFC] gas emitted yearly in the US. The production and release of CFC gas is now banned internationally by the Montreal Protocol because it is the main culprit responsible for stratospheric ozone depletion. But CFC is also a global warmer, 10,000 to 20,000 times more potent than carbon dioxide.

In fact, the nuclear fuel cycle utilises large quantities of fossil fuel at all of its stages—the mining and milling of uranium, the construction of the nuclear reactor and cooling towers, robotic decommissioning of the intensely radioactive reactor at the end of its 20 to 40-year operating lifetime, and transportation and long-term storage of massive quantities of radioactive waste.

In summary, nuclear power produces, according to a 2004 study by Jan Willem Storm van Leeuwen and Philip Smith, only three times fewer greenhouse gases than modern natural-gas[-fueled] power stations.

Nuclear Security

Nuclear plants currently operate at 64 sites in 31 states. Considering the devastation that could result from a successful terrorist attack on a nuclear plant, ensuring their protection should be a priority in a post-September 11 environment. However, the U.S. Nuclear Regulatory Commission (NRC) and nuclear industry are leaving plants vulnerable.

Public Citizen, *"The Case Against Nuclear Power,"* 2006.

Nuclear Power Is Not Clean Power

Contrary to the nuclear industry's propaganda, nuclear power is therefore not green and it is certainly not clean. Nuclear reactors consistently release millions of curies of radioactive isotopes into the air and water each year. These releases are unregulated because the nuclear industry considers these particular radioactive elements to be biologically inconsequential. This is not so.

These unregulated isotopes include the noble gases krypton, xenon and argon, which are fat-soluble and if inhaled by persons living near a nuclear reactor, are absorbed through the lungs, migrating to the fatty tissues of the body, including the abdominal fat pad and upper thighs, near the reproductive organs. These radioactive elements, which emit high-energy gamma radiation, can mutate the genes in the eggs and sperm and cause genetic disease.

Tritium, another biologically significant gas, is also routinely emitted from nuclear reactors. Tritium is composed of three atoms of hydrogen, which combine with oxygen, forming radioactive water, which is absorbed through the skin, lungs and digestive system. It is incorporated into the DNA molecule, where it is mutagenic.

The dire subject of massive quantities of radioactive waste accruing at the 442 nuclear reactors across the world is also rarely, if ever, addressed by the nuclear industry. Each typical 1000-megawatt nuclear reactor manufactures 33 tonnes of thermally hot, intensely radioactive waste per year.

Already more than 80,000 tonnes of highly radioactive waste sits in cooling pools next to the 103 US nuclear power plants, awaiting transportation to a storage facility yet to be found. This dangerous material will be an attractive target for terrorist sabotage as it travels through 39 states on roads and railway lines for the next 25 years.

But the long-term storage of radioactive waste continues to pose a problem. The US Congress in 1987 chose Yucca Mountain in Nevada, 150km northwest of Las Vegas, as a repository for America's high-level waste. But Yucca Mountain has subsequently been found to be unsuitable for the long-term storage of high-level waste because it is a volcanic mountain made of permeable pumice stone and it is transected by 32 earthquake faults. A congressional committee discovered fabricated data about water infiltration and cask corrosion in Yucca Mountain that had been produced by personnel in the US Geological Survey. These startling revelations, according to most experts, have almost disqualified Yucca Mountain as a waste repository, meaning that the US now has nowhere to deposit its expanding nuclear waste inventory.

To make matters worse, a study release [in April 2005] by the National Academy of Sciences shows that the cooling pools at nuclear reactors, which store 10 to 30 times more radioactive material than that contained in the reactor core, are subject to catastrophic attacks by terrorists, which could unleash an inferno and release massive quantities of deadly radiation—significantly worse than the radiation released by Chernobyl, according to some scientists.

This vulnerable high-level nuclear waste contained in the cooling pools at 103 nuclear power plants in the US includes hundreds of radioactive elements that have different biological impacts on the human body, the most important being cancer and genetic diseases.

The incubation time for cancer is five to 50 years following exposure to radiation. It is important to note that children, old people and immuno-compromised individuals are many times more sensitive to the malignant effects of radiation than [are] other people.

Dangerous Elements

I will describe four of the most dangerous elements made in nuclear power plants.

Iodine 131, which was released at the nuclear accidents at Sellafield in Britain, Chernobyl in Ukraine and Three Mile Island in the US, is radioactive for only six weeks and it bioconcentrates in leafy vegetables and milk. When it enters the human body via the gut and the lung, it migrates to the thyroid gland in the neck, where it can later induce thyroid cancer. In Belarus more than 2000 children have had their thyroids removed for thyroid cancer, a situation never before recorded in pediatric literature.

Strontium 90 lasts for 600 years. As a calcium analogue, it concentrates in cow and goat milk. It accumulates in the human breast during lactation, and in bone, where it can later induce breast cancer, bone cancer and leukemia.

Cesium 137, which also lasts for 600 years, concentrates in the food chain, particularly meat. On entering the human body, it locates in muscle, where it can induce a malignant muscle cancer called a sarcoma.

Plutonium 239, one of the most dangerous elements known to humans, is so toxic that one-millionth of a gram is carcinogenic. More than 200kg is made annually in each 1000-megawatt nuclear power plant. Plutonium is handled like iron in the body, and is therefore stored in the liver, where it causes liver cancer, and in the bone, where it can induce bone cancer and blood malignancies. On inhalation it causes lung cancer. It also crosses the placenta, where, like the drug thalidomide, it can cause severe congenital deformities. Plutonium has a predisposition for the testicle, where it can cause testicular cancer and induce genetic diseases in future generations. Plutonium lasts for 500,000 years, living on to induce cancer and genetic diseases in future generations of plants, animals and humans.

Plutonium is also the fuel for nuclear weapons—only 5kg is necessary to make a bomb and each reactor makes more than 200kg per year. Therefore any country with a nuclear power plant can theoretically manufacture 40 bombs a year.

Toxic Legacy

Because nuclear power leaves a toxic legacy to all future generations, because it produces global warming gases, because it is far more expensive than any other form of electricity generation, and because it can trigger proliferation of nuclear weapons, these topics need urgently to be introduced into the . . . educational system.

> *"Nuclear energy . . . remains the only practical, safe and environmentally-friendly means of reducing greenhouse gas emissions and addressing energy security."*

Nuclear Power Is a Safe Alternative to Fossil Fuels

Patrick Moore

Patrick Moore, chairman and chief scientist of Greenspirit Strategies, was a founder of the environmental activist group Greenpeace—which opposes the use of nuclear energy—in the 1960s. In the following excerpt from his congressional testimony in April 2005, Moore explains his revised position that the benefits of nuclear power have been shown to outweigh the risks. He states that environmentalists should support nuclear energy as a practical alternative to fossil fuels to reduce global warming and to meet growing global demand for electricity.

As you read, consider the following questions:

1. What evidence does Moore give that nuclear power is not environmentally harmful?
2. According to the author, why should there be a much greater emphasis on renewable energy production?

Patrick Moore, "Statement to the Congressional Subcommittee on Energy and Resources," www.nei.org, April 25, 2005. Reproduced by permission of the author.

3. What does Moore cite as additional benefits of nuclear energy?

I believe the majority of environmental activists, including those at Greenpeace, have now become so blinded by their extremist policies that they fail to consider the enormous and obvious benefits of harnessing nuclear power to meet and secure America's growing energy needs. These benefits far outweigh the risks.

There is now a great deal of scientific evidence showing nuclear power to be an environmentally sound and safe choice.

The Current Situation

Today nuclear energy supplies 20 per cent of US electrical energy.

Yet demand for electricity continues to rise and in the coming decades may increase by 50 per cent over current levels.

If nothing is done to revitalize the US nuclear industry, the industry's contribution to meeting US energy demands could drop from 20 per cent to 9 per cent.

What sources of energy would make up the difference?

It is virtually certain that the only technically feasible path is an even greater reliance on fossil fuels.

The Business as Usual Scenario Does Not Work

In a 'business as usual' scenario a significant reduction in greenhouse gas emissions (GHG) seems unlikely given our continued heavy reliance on fossil fuels. An investment in nuclear energy would go a long way to reducing this reliance and could actually result in reduced CO_2 emissions from power generation.

According to the Clean Air Council, annual power plant emissions are responsible for 36% of carbon dioxide (CO_2),

64% of sulfur dioxide (SO_2), 26% of nitrogen oxides (NO_x), and 33% of mercury emissions (Hg).

These four pollutants cause significant environmental impact, including acid rain, smog, respiratory illness, mercury contamination, and are the major contributors to GHG emissions.

Among power plants, old coal-fired plants produce the majority of these pollutants. By contrast, nuclear power plants produce an insignificant quantity of these pollutants. According to the Clean Air Council, while 58% of power plant boilers in operation in the U.S. are fueled by coal, they contribute 93% of NO_x, 96% of SO_2, 88% of CO_2, and 99% of the mercury emitted by the entire power industry.

Nuclear Energy Solution

Prominent environmental figures like Stewart Brand, founder of the *Whole Earth Catalog*, Gaia theorist James Lovelock, and Hugh Montefiore, former Friends of the Earth leader, have now all stated their strong support for nuclear energy as a practical means of reducing greenhouse gas emissions while meeting the world's increasing energy demands.

I too place myself squarely in that category.

UK environmentalist James Lovelock, who posited the Gaia theory that the Earth operates as a giant, self-regulating super-organism, now sees nuclear energy as key to our planet's future health. "Civilization is in imminent danger," he warns, "and has to use nuclear—the one safe, available energy source—or suffer the pain soon to be inflicted by our outraged planet."

While I may not be quite so strident as my friend James Lovelock, it is clear that whatever risk there is from increased CO_2 levels in the atmosphere—and there may be considerable risk—can be offset by an emphasis on nuclear energy.

In . . . the Massachusetts Institute of Technology's *Technology Review*, Stewart Brand writes that nuclear energy's problems can be overcome and that:

> "The industry is mature, with a half-century of experience and ever improved engineering behind it. Problematic early reactors like the ones at Three Mile Island and Chernobyl can be supplanted by new, smaller-scale, meltdown-proof reactors like the ones that use the pebble-bed design. Nuclear power plants are very high yield, with low-cost fuel. Finally, they offer the best avenue to a 'hydrogen economy,' combining high energy and high heat in one place for optimal hydrogen generation."

Nuclear Power Is a Proven Alternative

Indeed, nuclear power is already a proven alternative to fossil fuels.

The United States relies on nuclear power for some 20% of its electricity production, and produces nearly one-third of global nuclear energy.

Despite its current limited supply, nuclear energy now provides the vast majority (76.2 per cent) of the US's emission-free generation. (Others include hydroelectric, geothermal, wind, biomass, and solar.)

In 2002, the use of nuclear energy helped the US avoid the release of 189.5 million tons of carbon into the air, if this electricity had been produced by coal.

In fact, the electric sector's carbon emissions would have been 29 per cent higher without nuclear power.

And while hydro, geothermal and wind energy all form an important part of reducing our reliance on fossil fuels, without nuclear energy that reliance will likely not diminish. In 2002, carbon emissions avoided by nuclear power were 1.7 times larger than those avoided by all renewables combined.

But let me make it clear at this point that I believe there should also be a much greater emphasis on renewable energy production. I believe the two most important renewable energy technologies are wind energy, which has great potential, and ground-source heat pumps, known as geothermal or GeoExchange. Solar panels will not be cost effective for mass application until their cost is reduced by 5–10 times. I would not be inclined to support an energy policy that focused exclusively on nuclear but would rather insist that an equal emphasis be placed on renewables, even though it is not possible, given present technologies, that renewables could produce the same quantity of power as nuclear plants.

More Nuclear Energy

Nuclear energy has already made a sizeable contribution to the reduction of GHG emissions in the US.

But more must be done and nuclear energy is pointing the way.

A revitalized American nuclear energy industry, producing an additional 10,000 MW [megawatts] from power plant upgrades, plant restarts and productivity gains could assist the electric sector to avoid the emission of 22 million metric tons of carbon per year by 2012, according to the Nuclear Energy Institute—that's 21 per cent of the President's GHG intensity reduction goal.

A doubling of nuclear energy production would make it possible to significantly reduce total GHG emissions nationwide.

While current investment in America's nuclear energy industry languishes, development of commercial plants in other parts of the world is gathering momentum.

In order to create a better environmental and energy secure future, the US must once again renew its leadership in this area.

Let's Go Nuclear

Nuclear certainly has problems—accidents, waste storage, high construction costs, and the possible use of its fuel in weapons. It also has advantages besides the overwhelming one of being atmospherically clean. The industry is mature, with a half-century of experience and ever improved engineering behind it. Problematic early reactors like the ones at Three Mile Island and Chernobyl can be supplanted by new, smaller-scale, meltdown-proof reactors like the ones that use the pebble-bed design. Nuclear power plants are very high yield, with low-cost fuel. Finally, they offer the best avenue to a "hydrogen economy," combining high energy and high heat in one place for optimal hydrogen generation.

Stewart Brand, "Environmental Heresies,"
Technology Review, *May 2005.*

Safety

As Stewart Brand and other forward-thinking environmentalists and scientists have made clear, technology has now progressed to the point where the activist fearmongering about the safety of nuclear energy bears no resemblance to reality.

The Chernobyl and Three Mile Island reactors, often raised as examples of nuclear catastrophe by activists, were very different from today's rigorously safe nuclear energy technology. Chernobyl was actually an accident waiting to happen: bad design, shoddy construction, poor maintenance and unprofessional operation all combined to cause the only terrible accident in reactor history. In my view the Chernobyl accident was the exception that proves the rule that nuclear reactors are generally safe. Three Mile Island was actually a success story in that the radiation from the partially melted core was contained by the concrete containment structure, it did the job it was designed to do.

Today, approximately one-third of the cost of a nuclear reactor is dedicated to safety systems and infrastructure. The Chernobyl reactor, for example, was not outfitted with the fully automated, multiple levels of safety and redundancy required for North American reactors.

As we speak there are over 100 nuclear reactors in the US and over 400 worldwide that are producing electricity every day without serious incident.

Nuclear Waste Can Be Securely Stored

The fact that reactors produce nuclear waste is often used to support opposition to them. First, there is no technical obstacle to keeping nuclear waste from entering the environment at harmful levels. Second, this is already being accomplished at hundreds of nuclear power sites around the world. It is simply an issue of secure containment and maintenance. Most important, the spent fuel from reactors still has over 95% of its potential energy contained within it. Therefore spent fuel should not be disposed of, it should be stored securely so that in the future we can use this energy productively.

Nuclear Proliferation

Nuclear reactors produce plutonium that can be extracted and manufactured into nuclear weapons. This is unfortunate but is not in itself justification for eliminating nuclear energy. It appears that the main technologies that have resulted in combat deaths in recent years are machetes, rifles, and car bombs. No one would seriously suggest banning machetes, guns, cars or the fertilizer and diesel that explosives are made from. Nuclear proliferation must be addressed as a separate policy issue from the production of nuclear energy.

Other Benefits

Besides reductions in GHG emissions and the shift away from our reliance on fossil fuels, nuclear energy offers two important additional and environmentally friendly benefits.

First, nuclear power offers an important and practical pathway to the proposed "hydrogen economy." Unfortunately there are no hydrogen mines where we can source this element directly. It must be manufactured, from fossil fuels, biomass, or by splitting water into hydrogen and oxygen. Splitting water is the only non-greenhouse gas emitting approach to manufacturing hydrogen.

Hydrogen, as a fuel, offers the promise of clean, green energy for our automobiles and transportation fleets.

Automobile manufacturers continue to improve hydrogen fuel cells and the technology may, in the not-too-distant future, become feasible for mass application.

By using electricity, or by using heat directly from nuclear reactors to produce hydrogen, it may be possible to move from fossil fuels for transport energy to using clean hydrogen, thus virtually eliminating smog caused by autos, trucks, and trains.

A hydrogen fuel cell-powered transport fleet would not only virtually eliminate CO_2 emissions but would eliminate the energy security problem posed by reliance on oil from overseas.

Second, around the world, nuclear energy could be used to solve another growing crisis: the increasing shortage of fresh water available for human consumption and crop irrigation.

By using nuclear energy, seawater could be desalinized to satisfy the ever-growing demand for fresh water without the CO_2 emissions caused by fossil fuel-powered plants.

Conclusion

I want to conclude by emphasizing that nuclear energy—combined with the use of renewable energy sources like wind, geothermal and hydro—remains the only practical, safe and environmentally-friendly means of reducing greenhouse gas emissions and addressing energy security.

If the US is to meet its ever-increasing demands for energy, while reducing the threat of climate change and reliance on overseas oil, then the American nuclear industry must be revitalized and permitted to grow.

The time for common sense and scientifically sound leadership on the nuclear energy issue is now.

"There have been many thousands of minor accidents in reactors around the world . . . as well as falsified safety reports at operating reactors."

Nuclear Power Is Not a Safe Alternative to Fossil Fuels

Harvey Blatt

In the following article, geologist Harvey Blatt argues that the dangers of radioactivity associated with nuclear power production, waste disposal, and accidents make nuclear power an unsafe energy source. Blatt portrays radioactive leaks and debris as a "biological time bomb," and the cause of a wide range of human cancers and multiple-species genetic mutations. According to Blatt, a major accident such as Chernobyl in 1986 is not the only scenario to worry about; he cites thirty thousand minor nuclear accidents in the United States since Three Mile Island in 1979. Harvey Blatt is professor of geology at the Institute of Earth Sciences at the Hebrew University of Jerusalem.

As you read, consider the following questions:

1. According to Blatt, what effect has the Chernobyl accident had on human liver, lung, and thyroid cancer rates?

Harvey Blatt, *America's Environmental Report Card*. Cambridge, MA: MIT Press, 2004. Copyright © 2004. Reproduced by permission of The MIT Press, Cambridge, MA.

2. What genetic mutations in wildlife species near nuclear power plants does Blatt blame on radioactivity leaks?

3. What evidence does the author cite that reactor structures are dangerously in need of repair?

> Nuclear fission energy is safe only if a number of critical devices work as they should, if a number of people in key positions follow all their instructions, if there is no sabotage, no hijacking of the transport, if no nuclear fuel processing plant or repository anywhere in the world is situated in a region of riots or guerrilla activity, and no revolution or war—even a "conventional" one—takes place in these regions. No acts of God can be permitted.
>
> —*Hannes Alfven, Nobel Laureate, Physics*

The central concern about nuclear power is the escape of radiation from the nuclear fuel. Cancer clusters have been found around nuclear plants worldwide. A U.S. government study found a high incidence of 22 different types of cancer at 14 different U.S. nuclear weapons facilities across the country. There is evidence that working in a nuclear plant affects both the body cells and sperm of male employees. There are also data indicating that there is a far higher than normal occurrence of cancers in children living near nuclear power plants, and that the number of new cancers drops dramatically when the plants are shut down. Added to this is the discovery of radioactive ants, roaches, rats, gnats, flies, worms, and pigeons near nuclear plants. And there have been many thousands of minor accidents in reactors around the world, 30,000 in the United States alone since the Three Mile Island accident 25 years ago, as well as falsified safety reports at operating reactors. Compounding this has been the tendency of the federal government to either underestimate the dangers of radioactivity or to deliberately conceal relevant facts. And then there are major accidents such as at Three Mile Island in 1979 and Chernobyl in 1986. Is it any wonder that a large percentage of the American population fears nuclear power?

Fears have heightened since the 9/11 terrorist attack on the World Trade Center and the nation's capital. A scientific investigation completed in January 2003 reported that a successful terrorist attack on a spent-fuel storage pool at a large nuclear reactor could have consequences significantly worse than Chernobyl. Because there is still no long-term storage site for nuclear fuel, the risk will persist even if the reactors where it is now stored were shut down. . . .

Lessons from Chernobyl

> I'm not worried. Soviet radiation is the best in the world.
>
> —*Russian worker at the Chernobyl nuclear plant*

The explosion of a nuclear reactor at 1:23 A.M. on April 26, 1986, at Chernobyl in a remote area in northern Ukraine, just south of the border with Belarus, was the worst accident in the history of nuclear power generation. The reactor experienced both a steam explosion and a partial meltdown of its nuclear core and released about 3 percent of its radioactive material. The roof blew off the reactor building and enormous volumes of radioactive dust were hurled into the atmosphere to drift over the entire Northern Hemisphere. Worst hit were Ukraine, Belarus, and Scandinavia, although all of Europe was affected. In Germany, the teeth of children born after the Chernobyl explosion contain ten times the amount of radioactive strontium as the teeth of children born before the explosion. In northeastern France, women's liver-cancer rates have gone up by 182 percent, lung cancer by 120 percent, and thyroid cancer by 283 percent in regions affected by Chernobyl fallout. Corresponding rates for men are 225 percent, 272 percent, and 86 percent. In France as a whole, thyroid cancers have doubled.

The scattered radioactive debris was and still is a biological time bomb whose full effects will not be known for perhaps a hundred years or more. As of 2000, at least 9,000 people have died from the accident. In heavily contaminated areas there has been a 12 percent increase in birth defects. Inherited genetic damage has been found in children born in 1995 to parents who were exposed to the fallout. These birth defects include polydactyly (extra fingers and toes), and shortened limbs. The damage is to DNA in both sperm and eggs. Such mutations become part of the genetic code and are passed down through the generations.

Health Problems

Ukraine and Belarus spend a substantial part of their national budgets dealing with health problems resulting from the Chernobyl fallout. There are 50 million people in Ukraine. As of 2000, 3.3 million of them (7 percent of the population!) have suffered illness as a result of the contamination, and the incidence of some types of cancer is 10 times the preexplosion average. According to the country's Deputy Health Minister in 2000, "The health of people affected by the Chernobyl accident is getting worse and worse every year." It is now 17 years since the disaster and the damage toll is still rising.

As of the end of 1998, 73,000 Ukrainians not yet killed by the disaster have been recognized by their government as being fully disabled by it, and another 323,000 adults and 1.1 million children are entitled to government aid for Chernobyl-related health problems. In 1996, 10 years after the disaster, Ukraine and Belarus still had 200 times more radiation in their affected areas than Hiroshima and Nagasaki had a decade after they were bombed to end World War II. The eventual death toll from the Chernobyl disaster will be in the millions over many decades.

The situation in now-bankrupt Belarus is equally horrifying. They received 70 percent of the radiation from the explosion in Ukraine, and the present state of the country is indicated by some population statistics. Belarus is the same size as the United Kingdom but has only 10 million people.

Only 1 percent of the country is totally free of contamination.

One-quarter of all prime farmland is contaminated and permanently out of production.

Over 50,000 children have thyroid disorders. Nine hundred die each year from thyroid cancer.

As many as 800,000 children are at high risk of contracting cancer or leukemia.

Ninety percent of mothers nursing at the time of the explosion were giving breast milk that was radioactive.

Ninety-two percent of children suffer from something related to Chernobyl.

Twenty-five percent of the state budget is spent alleviating the after effects of Chernobyl.

Increase in Thyroid Cancer

Much worldwide publicity has attended the sharp increase in thyroid cancer among children in Ukraine and Belarus affected by the Chernobyl explosion. Noticeably increased rates of this disease occur more than 200 miles from the explosion; more than 50,000 children suffer from thyroid problems and about 3 percent of them have thyroid cancer, a disease that occurs spontaneously in only one in a million children. The incidence is most severe among children who were under 4 years old at the time of the disaster; more than one-third of them are expected to develop thyroid cancer. The average length of time for thyroid cancer to emerge is 17 years after exposure—that is, in 2003. The World Health Organization predicts at least another 50,000 cases of thyroid cancer in the coming years. The explosion released large amounts of radioactive iodine-131, an element absorbed by the thyroid gland to manufacture thyroid hormone. Thyroid cancer is treatable and most of the children will survive, although their thyroid gland will need to be surgically removed and they will need thyroid-hormone replacements for the rest of their lives.

A Troubling Prospect

It is easy to imagine why the prospect of a fleet of aging nuclear power plants would be troubling to many people. Every existing plant is approaching the end of its expected lifecycle—the time when a plant is as likely to experience serious accidents and failures as when it first became operational. If the NRC's [Nuclear Regulatory Commission's] past is any indication of its future, effective monitoring of aging plants is at best unlikely. As Anna Aurilio, staff scientist for the U.S. Public Interest Research Group, puts it, "Throughout the NRC's history, promoting nuclear power has been a higher priority than regulating it."

Without an effective regulator, keeping existing reactors running beyond their expected lifetimes creates grave risks for public health and safety. The public needs the NRC to be a vigilant supervisor of aging plants and to close those plants where safety problems outweigh the benefits of continued operation. The agency's dismal track record, however, does not instill confidence. For now, the future of nuclear power in the United States does not look very bright.

Eric Young, "The Risk of a Lifetime," Catalyst, Fall 2004.

As a result of the Ukrainian experience with thyroid cancer, France—the country that depends most heavily on nuclear power—has handed out potassium iodide pills to 600,000 people living within 6 miles of a nuclear plant. The French government has about 2 million of the pills stockpiled in a warehouse just north of Paris. Austria and Switzerland also have iodine distribution programs. Swallowing these pills within a few hours of exposure to radioactive iodine can saturate the thyroid gland with nonradioactive iodine so it will not absorb the radioactive stuff. France's distribution program can only be viewed as political, since radioactive contamination spread more than a thousand miles from Chernobyl. Children living within 6 miles of a nuclear plant are hardly more at risk than those living 60 miles away. The World Health Organization has recommended that all schoolchildren in Europe have immediate access to potassium iodide pills in the event of a nuclear accident.

U.S. Stockpiles Potassium Iodide Pills

In 1998 the U.S. Nuclear Regulatory Commission said it would encourage states that house the nation's nuclear power plants to stockpile potassium iodide pills. Late in 2001 the federal government bought 1.6 million of the pills and bought at least 6 million more in 2002. Following the terrorist attack on the World Trade Center in 2001, California decided to give potassium iodide pills to everyone living within 10 miles of a nuclear power plant. The nightmare continues.

The Minister of Agriculture in Ukraine, a grain-growing breadbasket country similar to the American Midwest, said in 1996, "We know this land should not be farmed, but if we don't ... we will simply starve." It will no doubt be many more decades before it will be safe to eat Ukrainian food. Grazing lands in faraway Scandinavia are still too radioactive to raise cattle and reindeer for human consumption. In December 2002, 16 years after the disaster, an atomic food inspector in Moscow, about 420 miles north of Chernobyl, noted that "there are practically no cases of radioactive watermelons this year." Now there's a minimum requirement for you!

Organisms in the soil have also been affected by the radioactivity that spewed from Chernobyl. Contaminated worms living within a few miles of the accident are now having sex with each other instead of on their own. Two species have switched from asexual to sexual reproduction. It is not known whether they will ever return to their former ways.

Radiation Effects Are Far-Reaching

Those directly in the path of radiation from the Chernobyl explosion were not the only ones affected by it. As of the end of 1998, 12 years after the disaster, a total of 4,365 "liquidators," the name Ukraine gave to those who took part in the Soviet cleanup effort, have died since 1986 of causes "directly linked" to their work at Chernobyl. In addition, endocrine disorders and stroke appear to be rising disproportionately among the roughly 650,000 liquidators assigned to the initial "cleanup" efforts; 70,000 have been disabled by the radiation. A recent study of liquidators' children conceived after the accident revealed they have seven times as many mutations as did their older siblings, a sign that radiation had damaged DNA in their parents' sperm and eggs. I would not want to be a worker at this job site. The radiation levels inside the reactor building are so high that plant employees joke that it's the biggest microwave in the world.

The reactor's shattered fuel elements and other highly radioactive debris were entombed by the liquidators in a hastily constructed steel and concrete sarcophagus, which is already cracked and leaking radioactivity. In April 2003, Russia's atomic energy minister noted that the coffin "has a lot of holes" and that "we can see a situation where the roof could fall in, or other supports that hold up the roof could fall down. There is a strong chance it could happen." Ukrainian officials agreed, noting that gaps in the shell totaled more than 10,500 square feet. They added: "The sarcophagus does not meet mechanical and structural safety requirements . . . thus there is a danger that part of the shelter could indeed collapse. It is a realistic possibility." Ukrainian and Western financial donors plan to build a new sarcophagus over the destroyed reactor. It should be completed in 2008. So far $11 billion have been spent on coping with the aftermath of the Chernobyl disaster.

The Russian-built reactors at Chernobyl are of a design not used in the United States, but 15 reactors of the same type are still in operation, 2 in Lithuania and 13 in Russia. Our reactors are considerably safer than those at Chernobyl. However, no one can guarantee that accidents caused by human error will not end in an American nuclear disaster. There have been a large number of serious nuclear calamities in recent years, the most newsworthy being the 1999 event at Tokiamura, Japan. Workers improperly handled uranium-235 and triggered a runaway chain reaction that burned uncontrolled for 20 hours. The International Atomic Energy Agency branded it the world's third worst nuclear accident behind the 1986 Chernobyl disaster and the 1979 event at Three Mile Island in Pennsylvania.

The Tokiamura, Japan, accident in 1999 unleashed radiation 20,000 times the normal level and injured at least 49 people, some critically. Local people were exposed to radiation levels estimated to be 100 times the annual safe limit. The effects of the radioactive rain that fell on the surrounding area have yet to be determined. Investigators have also found higher than expected uranium concentrations in the site environment, possibly indicating prior, unreported accidents. The Sumitomo Metal Mining Company was found guilty in 2003 of causing the Tokiamura accident and was fined $8,000. It voluntarily closed its nuclear-fuel-processing business. Six employees found guilty of causing the accident were given suspended prison sentences.

Despite the Tokiamura incident, the Japanese government seems inconsistent in its concern about the safety of its reactors. On the one hand, Tokyo Electric Power (Tepko) the world's biggest private electricity supplier, has closed 17 nuclear power plants because of safety concerns. On the other hand, in a nuclear reactor at Shika on the northern peninsula of Ishikawa, 249 cracks have been found in a reactor shroud containing the main coolant and a small amount of water has leaked out. The Japanese nuclear regulator says no repairs are needed. Perhaps more frightening was the admission by two power companies that they had neglected to report signs of reactor cracks first noticed in September 1998. And in August 2002 General Electric International, which built and maintains many of Tepko's plants, admitted that it had falsified safety records at 37 locations. What do you believe should be the punishment for such dangerous and unconscionable behavior?

Cracks have also been found in the nozzles on the lids of 14 reactors in the United States. The lids are being replaced at a cost of $25 million each. In April 2003, leaks were found at the bottom of a Texas reactor's pressure vessel, a site much harder to repair than leaks in the lid. It's getting harder to sleep at night.

Eastern Europe and the countries of the former Soviet Union contain 57 operating nuclear reactors that are not safe enough to be licensed in the United States. The countries housing these unsafe reactors are aware of their unsafe nature but do not have the money to do anything about it. The wealthier nations must do most of the paying to improve these reactors because, as Chernobyl demonstrated, *a nuclear accident anywhere is a nuclear accident everywhere.*

> *"Casks, centrally located, could make the high-level-waste problem a lot easier to solve and increase national security much sooner."*

Nuclear Waste Can Be Handled Safely

Matthew L. Wald

In the following article, journalist Matthew L. Wald argues that the debate over nuclear waste storage is too fixated on daunting long-term solutions, and that safe, available short-term solutions are actually sufficient. In particular, he advocates placing nuclear waste in specially designed concrete-and-steel casks, stored above-ground in a central location for fifty to one hundred years. By that time, Wald suggests, spent reactor fuel will be much less radioactive and easier to handle, and future generations are likely to have new and better ideas for continued storage. Matthew L. Wald, a reporter for the New York Times *Washington bureau, has written about the nuclear industry for twenty-five years.*

As you read, consider the following questions:

1. According to Wald, what are the advantages of storing nuclear waste in casks instead of the Yucca Mountain facility?

2. How would the technology of electrometallurgical reprocessing reduce the quantity of nuclear waste and make it less dangerous, according to Wald?

3. What knowledge and possible improvements in storage technology does the author suggest could be available in fifty to a hundred years?

When American Airlines Flight 11 flew at low altitude down the Hudson River valley on the morning of Sept. 11, 2001, its target was the north tower of the World Trade Center. But its impact is still being felt at a cluster of buildings it passed about five minutes before it reached lower Manhattan, at a nuclear-reactor complex called Indian Point in Buchanan, NY. Adjacent to the site's two operating reactors are two buildings packed with highly radioactive spent-fuel rods, in pools of water 12 meters deep and tinged Ty-D-Bol blue by boron added to tamp down nuclear chain reactions. The soothing hum of the pumps that circulate the building's warm, moist air—and, critically, keep the water cool—lends an atmosphere of industrial tranquility.

Without that cooling water, the fuel cladding might overheat, melt, catch fire, and release radiation. Whether the impact of a Boeing 767 like Flight 11 could drain one of the pools and disable backup water pumps, starting such a fire, is far from clear. Nevertheless, the threat of terrorism in general and the flyover of Flight 11 in particular have reignited the debate about why all of this dangerous fuel is still here— indeed, why all spent fuel produced at Indian Point in three decades is still here—and not at Yucca Mountain, the federal government's burial spot near Las Vegas, where it was supposed to be shipped beginning [in 1998].

[In late summer 2004] a construction project began at Indian Point that will allow the fuel to be pulled out of the pools. But it's not going to Yucca. The government says Yucca won't be ready until 2010. Executives in the nuclear industry say a more likely date is between 2015 and never. So instead of traveling to Nevada, Indian Point's fuel is traveling about 100 meters, to a bluff overlooking the Hudson River. On a late-summer day [in 2004], a backhoe tore out maple and black-walnut trees to make way for a concrete pad. Beginning in 2005 the first of a planned 72 six-meter-tall concrete-and-steel casks will be placed there, a configuration that adds storage capacity and thus allows the twin power plants to keep operating. Though they provide a hedge against a worst-case fuel-pool meltdown, these casks are merely another temporary solution. The fact that they're needed at all represents the colossal failure of the U.S. Department of Energy's Yucca plans and technology.

Yet as engineering and policy failures go, this one has a silver lining. Conventional thinking holds that Yucca's problems must be solved quickly so that nuclear waste can be squirreled away safely and permanently, deep within a remote mountain. But here's the twist: with nuclear waste, procrastination may actually pay. The construction of cask fields presents a chance to rethink the conventional. The passage of several decades while the waste sits in casks could be immensely helpful. A century would give the United States time to observe progress on waste storage in other countries. In the meantime, natural radioactive decay would make the waste cooler and thus easier to deal with. What's more, technological advances over the next century might yield better long-term storage methods. "If it goes on for another 50 years, it doesn't matter. It could go on for 100 or 200 years, and it's probably for the better," says Allison Macfarlane, a geologist at MIT [the Massachusetts Institute of Technology] and coeditor of a forthcoming book on Yucca. "We've got plenty of time to play with it."

The government must now accept that its Yucca plan is a failure and that casks are the de facto solution. Indian Point's cask pad will not be the first; about two dozen operating reactors have them already. Others are likely to soon join the list.

And some casks—at Rowe, MA; Wiscasset, ME; Charlevoix, MI; and a site near Sacramento, CA—are nuclear orphans, having outlived their reactors. Each cask pad is roughly the size of a football field, floodlit, watched by motion sensors and closed-circuit TV, and surrounded by razor wire and armed guards. Given the homeland-security concern posed by nuclear-waste facilities, and the need to guard them individually, do we really want 60 of them—serving all 125 commercial reactors that have ever operated—to rise around the nation, many near population centers? If casks are the solution for the next generation or two, they should be put in one place.

Yucca is already on tenuous ground; in July 2004 a federal appeals court said that to open the mountain burial site, the government would have to show that it could contain waste for hundreds of thousands of years. Extensive scientific analyses by the Energy Department show it cannot. The court's decision throws the whole question back to the U.S. Congress, which must now decide whether to proceed with Yucca at all. This presents an opportunity to align policy with physics and abandon the Yucca-or-bust dogma that has dominated the debate for nearly 20 years. Casks, centrally located, could make the high-level-waste problem a lot easier to solve and increase national security much sooner, too.

Tunnel Vision

The federal fixation on Yucca Mountain now spans two decades. Beginning in the early 1980s, the government agreed to take waste from any nuclear utility that paid a tariff of a tenth of a cent per kilowatt-hour generated by its reactors. All the companies quickly signed up. But the selection of Yucca, 150 kilometers northwest of Las Vegas, was never driven by science. The site was chosen by that august group of geologists and physicists, the U.S. Congress. So far, the Energy Department has spent about $6 billion on development, including building an eight-kilometer, U-shaped tunnel through the mountain, in some places nearly 300 meters below the surface. It plans to spend at least $50 billion more to build dozens of side tunnels, package the waste in steel containers that look like the tanker portion of a gasoline track, place the waste in the tunnels, and operate the site for 50 to 100 years before sealing it for eternity. Problems have plagued Yucca since the beginning. . . .

Early in 2004 researchers at Catholic University of America, hired by the state of Nevada, took samples of the kind of metal the Energy Department wants to use at Yucca and put them in some water mixed with the minerals present in the mountain. As a series of speakers lectured reporters on why Yucca was a bad idea, the researchers sautéed the metal over a burner. By the time the lectures were done, the samples had corroded, some of them all the way through. How faithfully the stunt reproduced the chemistry of Yucca Mountain is debatable. But clearly, Yucca is subject to serious doubts. "You have to think [that] somewhere back in the premise structure of the whole thing, something was dreadfully wrong," says Stewart Brand, a San Francisco-based consultant who once advised the Canadian government on what to do with its own waste.

Cooler Fuel

The argument against casks is that they are merely temporary, not meant to serve longer than perhaps 100 years, and that they are a kind of surrender, leaving this generation's waste problem to a future generation to solve. Yet their impermanence is exactly what's good about them. A century hence, spent reactor fuel will be cooler and more amenable to permanent disposal. In fact, within a few decades, the average fuel bundle's heat output will be down to two or three hair dryers. After 150 years, only one-thirty-second of the cesium and strontium will remain. The remaining material can be buried closer together without boiling underground water. Reduced heat means reduced uncertainty.

Granted, spent fuel will be far from safe after such a relatively short period. Even after 100 years, it will still be so radioactive that a few minutes of direct exposure will be lethal. "It's many, many, many thousands of years before it's a no nevermind," says Geoffrey Schwartz, the cask manager for Indian Point, which is owned by Entergy Nuclear. "But the spent fuel does become more benign as time goes by."

The fuel could be more valuable, too. For decades, industry and government officials have recognized that "spent" reactor fuel contains a large amount of unused uranium, as well as another very good reactor fuel, plutonium, which is produced as a by-product of running the reactor. Both can be readily extracted, although right now the price of new uranium is so low, and the cost of extraction so high, that reprocessing spent fuel is not practical. And the political climate does not favor a technology that makes potential bomb fuel— plutonium—an item of international commerce. But things might be different in 100 years. For starters, the same fuel could be reprocessed much more easily, since the potentially valuable components will be in a matrix of material that is not so intensely radioactive.

And in 100 years, advances in reprocessing technology might make the economics compelling. The existing American technology dates from the Cold War and involves elaborate chemical steps that create vast quantities of liquid waste. But an alternative exists: electrometallurgical reprocessing. Though research into the technique has lagged of late because of the economic climate, the concept might be taken more seriously in the future. Electrodes could sort out the garbage (the atoms formed when uranium is split) from the usable uranium (the uranium-235 still available for fission and the uranium-238 that can be turned into plutonium in a reactor), in something

Official Support for the Cask Solution

[On December 16, 2005], U.S. Senators Harry Reid and John Ensign introduced legislation . . . mandating that nuclear waste be stored on-site where it is produced and requiring the federal government to take responsibility for possession, stewardship, maintenance, and monitoring of the waste. . . .

"The Yucca Mountain project is never going to open," Reid, the Senate Democratic Leader, said. "It is time we put the safety of this country first and approach the storage of nuclear waste in a way that is productive and realistic. There cannot be any weak links in the chain of security of our nation's nuclear power infrastructure. Storing nuclear waste on-site is the safest, most reasonable and most effective way of allowing nuclear power companies to continue operating while keeping the health and safety of Americans as our top priority."

"What we are proposing today represents the safest and most responsible course of action available for storing nuclear waste," Ensign said. "The dry cask storage technology exists to provide a viable, on-site alternative to shipping waste across the country."

Harry Reid and John Ensign,
"Reid, Ensign Introduce Nuclear Waste On-Site Storage Legislation,"
December 16, 2005. http://reid.senate.gov/.

like the way jewelers use electrometallurgy to apply silver plate. Resulting waste volumes would be far smaller.

Perhaps most importantly, in 100 years, energy supply and demand might be very different. Reprocessed nuclear fuel might well become a critical part of the energy supply, if the world has run out of cheap oil and we decide that burning coal is too damaging to our atmosphere. If that happens, we might have 1,000 nuclear reactors. On the other hand, we might have no reactors, depending on the progress of alternate energy sources like solar and wind. At this point, it's hard to tell, but we are not required to make the decision now; we can put the spent fuel in casks for 50 years and then decide if it is wheat or chaff.

There is a final, more practical reason that we might choose to take the plutonium out of spent fuel for reactor use: it makes the remainder easier to store. For the most part, what's left will not be radioactive for nearly as long, and the sheer volume of material will be lower. Mark Deinert, a physicist at Cornell University, says reprocessing, like recycling, removes about half of the material from the waste, dramatically decreasing storage costs and effectively doubling the capacity of a facility like Yucca.

Betting on Better Storage

While nuclear waste would be easier to handle in 50 or 100 years, it would still require isolation for several hundred thousand years. But there is every reason to expect that storage technology will improve in the next century. When we decide to permanently dispose of the waste, either after reprocessing or without reprocessing, we may be smarter at metallurgy, geology, and geochemistry than we are now.

Today, the basic technology at Yucca is a stainless-steel material called alloy 22, covered with an umbrella of titanium—a "drip shield" against water percolating down through the tunnel roof. That could look as primitive in 100 years as the Wright brothers' 1903 Flyer looks to us in 2004. Or it might simply be obsolete. Space-launch technology could become as reliable as jet airplanes are today, giving us a nearly foolproof way to throw waste into solar orbit. The mysteries of geochemistry might be as transparent as the human genetic code is becoming, which would mean we could say with confidence what kind of package would keep the waste encased for the next few hundred thousand years.

Or there might be easier ways to process the waste. For example, particle accelerators, routinely used to make medical isotopes, could provide a means to make the waste more benign. The principle has already been demonstrated experimentally: firing subatomic particles at high-level radioactive waste can change long-lived radioactive materials to short-lived ones. Richard A. Meserve, a former chairman of the U.S. Nuclear Regulatory Commission and now the chairman of a National Academy of Sciences panel on nuclear waste, says this technology, known as transmutation, might become more practical in 100 years. The technology of accelerators has advanced in the last few years, he says, and it is a good bet that it will continue to do so.

Some alternative storage technologies may need only a few more years of research and development. One is ceramic packaging. Ceramics have good resistance to radiation and heat, and they don't rust. At the moment, nobody casts ceramics big enough to hold fuel assemblies, which are typically about four meters long. But there is no theoretical limit to the sizes of ceramics; there has simply been no economic incentive to make giant ones. Nor will there be, until the only likely customer for them, the Energy Department, decides that the metal it is shopping for now isn't up to the job.

Another alternative calls for mixing waste with ceramics or minerals to form a rock-like material comprising about 20 percent waste. The waste would be chemically bound up in stable materials that are not prone to react with water. With a few decades' grace time, engineers could build samples and test them in harsh environments. But even though the idea has been around for more than 10 years, no one has put serious research money into it, since its only possible American customer, the Energy Department, has been committed to Yucca.

That situation shows no sign of change. The Energy Department, following Congress's orders, has so far declined to consider alternatives. Man-Sung Yim, a nuclear researcher at North Carolina State University in Raleigh, argues that some of these technologies are already mature but have been shoved aside in the Energy Department's rush, possibly futile, to open Yucca. "My reading at this point is, people working at the Yucca Mountain project office do not really want to change the design. The more change you bring in, the more delayed the processes," Yim says. "It's a pity, because we could make it better."

Central Casking

But the pursuit of the perfect solution (assuming deep geologic disposal even could be perfected) has ignored a realistic solution. And when the perfect fails, as now seems likely, we will be left with something no rational person would have chosen: waste sites scattered from coast to coast, in places where reactors used to be, each with its own security force, maintenance crew, and exclusion zone. "We're here to run a business as efficiently as possible," says John Sanchez, the project manager who oversaw the planning for the pad at Indian Point when he worked at Consolidated Edison, the site's former owner. "In a perfect world, you would not have 60 of anything, if you could have one." But after 20 years of pursuing geologic disposal, and 15 years of chasing Yucca and avoiding any mention of a plan B, just such an ad hoc, and suboptimal, solution is emerging.

And it's emerging without the support of the Energy Department. Testifying before the Senate Energy Committee in 2004, Kyle McSlarrow, the Energy Department's deputy secretary, said that "continued progress toward establishing a high-level waste repository at the Yucca Mountain site is absolutely essential." He told another committee on the same day that with progress toward Yucca's opening, "industry saw clearly that the nuclear-power option was truly back on the table."

. . .

Cask storage is not pretty, but what's wrong with the idea of an industrial repository, a few hectares set aside for the next century or so, a single, guarded location in a little-populated area, a location that in ten years or so will be remarkable only because it's a place where the snow doesn't stick? Macfarlane of MIT says making such a site secure and terrorist-proof would cost $6.5 billion, at most. "Isn't that worth it? How much have we spent on Iraq? Look what we got for that money. And there's more at risk here," she says.

> "[High-level nuclear waste] delivers a lethal dose in seconds and will remain a hazard for at least 12,000 human generations."

Nuclear Waste Cannot Be Handled Safely

Mary Olson

In the following viewpoint, Mary Olson argues that radioactive nuclear waste is a grave threat whether it is stored on-site, transported to the underground Yucca Mountain facility, or subjected to new reprocessing technologies. She challenges portrayals of reprocessing as recycling and asserts that it does not reduce radioactivity or waste volume. Mary Olson, director of the southeast office of the Nuclear Information and Resource Service in Washington, D.C., writes and speaks on nuclear waste disposal and storage issues.

As you read, consider the following questions:

1. How is nuclear waste more dangerous than the uranium fuel from which it is produced, according to Olson?

2. How does reprocessing destabilize nuclear waste, according to the author?

3. Why does Olson say the end product of reprocessing, MOX, is not a usable reactor fuel?

Every nuclear power reactor annually generates 20–30 tons of high-level nuclear waste since the irradiated fuel itself is the waste when removed from the reactor core. Like fuel, the waste is a solid ceramic pellet, stacked inside a thin metal tube or 'cladding.' In addition to residual uranium, the waste is about 1% plutonium that is formed inside the fuel rods by the reactor. The waste also contains about 5% highly radioactive fission products like cesium, strontium and iodine, making it millions of times more radioactive than "fresh" uranium fuel. Unshielded, it delivers a lethal dose in seconds and will remain a hazard for at least 12,000 human generations.

No End in Site

High-level waste is piling up at reactor sites, stored outside of containment in pools, and in large, dry containers called casks. A growing security threat, storage has been repeatedly approved to enable continued reactor operation, and therefore continued nuclear waste production, making risks greater. Now new reactors are being proposed, even though there is no credible solution for the approximately 120,000 tons of waste the first generation of reactors will produce.

The U.S. Department of Energy (DOE) has devoted nearly 20 years to the development of a high-level dump at Yucca Mountain, a geologically unstable, sacred site of the Western Shoshone people in Nevada. The State of Nevada and the Shoshone Nation have vigorously opposed this dump. Growing evidence substantiates that the Yucca site will fail in the fundamental goal of a repository: to isolate radioactivity from our environment. A second, industry-owned, alternative for centralizing the waste on an Indian Reservation in Utah led by a consortium called Private Fuel Storage (PFS) is meeting enduring opposition from that state. Both Yucca and PFS would trigger a "Mobile Chernobyl"—the largest nuclear waste shipping campaign in history—with so many transport miles that accidents are inevitable and security is an oxymoron.

Disregarding Hard-Won Wisdom

The [George W.] Bush/[Dick] Cheney administration and its congressional allies are intent on reversing over 30 years of extraordinarily rare common sense in nuclear policy. In the 1970s it was decided that irradiated fuel and the plutonium it contains should be treated as *waste*—not as a resource. This was in part due to the catastrophic failure after only one year of operations at West Valley, New York—the only commercial reprocessing site to operate in the U.S. West Valley's reprocessing mess is still not cleaned up—and the projected cost is over $5 billion.

Every reprocessing site (France, UK, Russia, and soon Japan have the largest sites) is an environmental catastrophe, with massive releases of radioactivity to air, land and water; high worker radiation exposures; and residues that are harder to handle than the terrible waste it begins with. Reprocessing creates stockpiles of nuclear weapons-usable plutonium, and is unviable without large taxpayer subsidies. President Jimmy Carter banned reprocessing as a nuclear non-proliferation measure; while Ronald Reagan lifted the ban, no commercial interest has pursued this expensive boondoggle, since it is not a profitable enterprise. Our current president apparently intends for taxpayers to pay for the relapse to reprocessing.

At the end of 2005, Congress awarded $50 million to the U.S. Department of Energy with instructions to make a new waste-reprocessing plan. DOE is directed to use one of its sites—in 2006 it was instructed to hold a "competition" and the "winner," to be announced in 2007, will get the new reprocessing site. Congress specified (another promise?) that the site should be opened by 2010.

Cartoon by Gary Oliver. Copyright © 1995 by G. Oliver for Big Bend Sentinel. Reproduced by permission.

[In the reprocessing sequence], the fuel rods are taken out of the assemblies, chopped up and then dissolved in nitric acid. The resulting highly radioactive and caustic stew is then processed to remove the plutonium and the uranium, leaving the highly radioactive fission products in the liquid. While there are methods to attempt to re-stabilize this material, there has been a fundamental loss in the stability of the dry ceramic pellet in the metal clad fuel rod.

Completely False Claims of Reprocessing

1. Reprocessing is NOT recycling. The formation of fission products in the fuel rods makes high-level waste fundamentally different from the uranium it came from. It is not possible to remake the original fuel again from high-level waste—thus it is not a cycle.

2. Reprocessing does not reduce radioactivity. No credible expert says reprocessing reduces total radioactivity; some less informed sources imply this. Reprocessing does not change the amount of radioactivity—except to smear it around a large surface area, thereby diluting it without any actual reduction of radioactivity.

3. Reprocessing does not reduce waste volume; to the contrary, fuel pellet volume is magnified by a factor of 100–100,000. The resulting "dilution" allows the reclassification from "high-level," to the so-called "low-level" waste category, which is still deadly.

The King Midas story of childhood teaches about the hazard of greed. Radioactive waste contaminates everything it comes in contact with—but instead of turning it all to gold, everything it comes in contact with is turned to expensive, dangerous radioactive waste!

A stated goal of reprocessing is to use plutonium for reactor fuel. The most common form is MOX (short for "mixed oxide"), made from plutonium and uranium 238 (depleted uranium). While today's reactors can use MOX fuel, it is both riskier and more hazardous: MOX is harder to control, and twice as deadly as uranium fuel if control is lost. MOX does not "solve" the waste problem since reprocessing MOX fuel is even harder than reprocessing uranium fuel, and not widely done. Princeton's Dr. Frank Von Hippel likens MOX use to "kicking the can down the road"—not dealing with the waste problem at all.

Plutonium Destabilizes Our World

High-level nuclear waste contains so much lethal radioactivity that the plutonium inside the waste fuel rods is effectively safeguarded. Separating out the plutonium makes it available for weapons use. For the United States to reverse more than 30 years of policy against recovering civil plutonium also reverses the moral authority with which the U.S. calls on other nations to refrain from this activity. North Korea and Iran are the most recent examples of countries ready to join the "nuclear weapons club." Reprocessing is a direct contradiction to US reprimands of these nations for nuclear proliferation. The clear intention of the Bush/Cheney team to return to full-scale production of new nuclear weapons adds to this atomic hypocrisy.

Far from putting the atomic genie back in the bottle, reprocessing creates millions of gallons of highly radioactive, caustic, destabilized high-level waste that history shows will leak; be evaporated; residues put into glass that may or may not retain the radioactivity for even a generation; and now, under a new policy, be left forevermore on the reprocessing site, mixed only with grout in a thin effort to keep it from contaminating soil, water, food and our bodies. This is NO SOLUTION.

Periodical Bibliography

The following articles have been selected to supplement the diverse views presented in this chapter.

Atlantic Monthly	"Nuclear Option," January/February 2005.
Geoffrey Colvin	"Nuclear Power Is Back—Not a Moment Too Soon," *Fortune*, May 30, 2005.
Jane Durney	"Nuclear Power in a Changing Climate," *Geography Review*, January 2005.
Economist	"British Dreams; Nuclear Power," May 21, 2005.
Perry A. Fischer	"Future Nuclear? New, but Not Clear," Editorial Comment, *World Oil Magazine*, September 2005. www.worldoil.com.
Mark Hertsgaard	"Nuclear Energy Can't Solve Global Warming: Other Remedies 7 Times More Beneficial," *San Francisco Chronicle*, August 7, 2005.
Chana R. Schoenberger	"Fear Factor," *Forbes*, July 26, 2004.
Lisa Stein	"A Nuclear Anniversary," *U.S. News & World Report*, April 5, 2004.
Mark Thompson and Bruce Crumley	"Are These Towers Safe? Why America's Nuclear Power Plants Are Still So Vulnerable to Terrorist Attack—and How to Make Them Safer," *Time*, June 20, 2005.
Polly Toynbee	"Capitulation to the Nuclear Lobby Is a Politics of Despair," *Guardian* (Manchester, UK), May 25, 2005. www.guardian.co.uk.
George Wehrfritz, Amy Webb, and Hideko Takayama	"Breach of Faith," *Newsweek International*, September 30, 2002.
Eric Young	"The Risk of a Lifetime," *Catalyst*, Fall 2004.

CHAPTER 3

What Renewable Energy Sources Should Be Developed?

Chapter Preface

Oil is a commodity like any other, subject to price swings depending on supply and demand, but throughout the twentieth century the price of crude oil to the U.S. petroleum industry was remarkably stable: Until 2000 the average price per barrel never exceeded $23.00 (in current dollars) except briefly in times of war in the Middle East. The situation has since changed drastically. Lowered production in Venezuela and Nigeria, the war in Iraq and geopolitical uncertainty over the oil supply elsewhere in the Persian Gulf, and shrinking gasoline inventories in the United States have contributed to skyrocketing oil prices: In April 2006 the price per barrel jumped above $72.00, and the average price of a gallon of gasoline in the United States reached $2.80 at the pump.

The unlikelihood that petroleum prices will fall significantly has led to renewed interest in a variety of alternative, renewable energy sources, including wind, solar energy, biofuels, ocean and tidal energy, and geothermal energy. Research and development is costly, however, and many Americans have criticized the Energy Policy Act of 2005 as a boost to oil and gas drilling ($2.6 billion allotted), coal ($2.9 billion allotted), and nuclear power plants ($3.1 billion allotted) at the expense of renewables. Out of a ten-year budget of $14.5 billion, renewable resources such as wind, biomass, geothermal, landfill gas, and hydropower together will receive tax credits of about $3.1 billion. The bill does set aside an additional $6 billion for new investments in ethanol plants.

Although the federal government is not leading the renewable energy effort, some states such as Maine are seeking to speed a transition to renewable energy sources by providing rebates and tax incentives for homeowners and businesses that install solar electric and solar hot water systems. Maine governor John E. Baldacci says, "The sun's power is free—imported oil is not. Solar electric and hot water systems can help insulate people from the tremendous price volatility Americans are seeing in world oil and gas markets. In addition, solar systems are produced in the United States, strengthening the economy and reducing our trade deficit."

Analysts disagree, however, about the ability of renewable energy resources such as wind and solar energy to meet the growing energy needs of either the United States or developing countries. Critics argue that renewables are neither efficient nor affordable: In Namibia, for example, most citizens are too poor to buy or install solar products available there.

Those who support renewables say that as long as the federal government is subsidizing the costs of oil and gas, coal, and nuclear power, the true costs of these nonrenewables will be masked and comparisons with renewables will be unfair. Renewable energy supporters also point to negative environmental and health effects from continued use of fossil fuels and nuclear power as an important reason to focus research on renewables.

In this chapter, experts debate what renewable resources should be pursued to counter the shortfall in petroleum resources, replace fossil fuels in the long term, and minimize environmental damage.

| *"Solar [power] will push the trend of safe, affordable, and reliable distributed energy."*

Solar Power Can Help Fuel the Future

Glenn Hamer

Glenn Hamer is the former executive director of the Solar Energy Industries Association in Washington, D.C. In the following excerpt, Hamer outlines the three primary types of solar energy, and suggests that solar power offers a reliable source of energy. He asserts that in addition to its benefit to the environment, solar energy technologies will also create new jobs for Americans, and will save consumers money.

As you read, consider the following questions:

1. What does the author indicate as the three primary types of solar energy?
2. How is solar energy well suited for heating water, according to the author?
3. According to the author, what benefits do zero net energy buildings offer consumers?

Glenn Hamer, "Solar Power 2002," *World & I*, vol. 17, June 2002. Copyright 2002 News World Communications, Inc. Reproduced by permission.

In the future, a larger percentage of the world's energy needs will be taken care of by solar devices that harness the heat and light provided by the sun. Solar energy can be used passively to generate heat or be converted directly to electricity by photovoltaic cells. Although solar collectors have been prohibitively expensive in the past, prices are falling. Americans should increase their reliance on this efficient, environmentally friendly energy source.

The forecast for solar energy in the twenty-first century is sunny. Solar will push the trend of safe, affordable, and reliable distributed energy. As we head deeper into the new century, some predict that the electricity system may come to resemble the Internet—with disparate points and no one center of activity. In such a system, photovoltaics integrated into building roofs and windows will be a key component. Especially in the Southwest, concentrating solar power (CSP) stations will provide a significant percentage of the energy.

The solar photovoltaics industry grew at an annual rate of over 20 percent worldwide in the past decade and 40 percent [between 2000–2002], reaching an annual photovoltaic module production of 100 megawatts (MW) in the United States and about 400 MW globally [a typical coal power plant produces 500 MW]. Worldwide in 2001, photovoltaics was a $2 billion business. In the United States alone, the industry employs about 20,000 people in high-value, high-tech jobs.

In the swimming pool sector of solar thermal, according to the Florida Solar Energy Center, the equivalent of 594 MW of power was installed in 2001 in the United States. For solar hot-water heating for general home use, one utility, Hawaii Electric, has installed systems that produce approximately 60 MW per year, and it continues to add around 12 MW of capacity annually.

Solar energy technologies are of three primary types: photovoltaics (PV), concentrating solar power (CSP), and solar thermal. Although all three aim to maximize the capture of usable energy from sunlight, their approaches are radically different. PV cells convert the energy of sunlight directly into electricity, while CSP converts concentrated heat energy from sunlight into electricity. Solar thermal uses sunlight's energy to heat water and buildings with no intermediate conversion to electricity.

Production Up, Costs Down

Manufacturing continues to expand in the United States and worldwide. As the industry has grown over the past 25 years, the cost of PV has declined by several orders of magnitude. The PV industry estimates that the system price paid by the end user will be $3–4 per watt in 2010 [compared with $7 to $10 per watt in 2004]. This power is being produced in the middle of the day, when electricity costs and needs are the highest. Furthermore, locally installed PV reduces stress on the transmission and distribution system.

Solar energy is especially well suited for heating water, a task that requires 15–20 percent of a home's total energy consumption. Solar water heaters can provide 50–90 percent of that hot water, and their original cost can be recovered through energy bill savings over the course of 4–7 years. Already, the most economical way to heat a pool is with solar. Today, 20 percent of all units sold to heat pools are solar. The potential value of the technology is shown in Israel, where solar hot water heaters displace 6 percent of the country's total electricity consumption.

Some of the distributed CSP technologies, such as roof-mounted systems, solar dishes, and concentrating PV, will also play a role in America's energy future.

According to the U.S. Photovoltaic Industry Roadmap, "The domestic photovoltaic industry will provide up to 15 percent (about 3,200 MW or 3.2 GW) of the new U.S. peak electricity generating capacity expected to be required in 2020." Cumulative U.S. PV shipments, both domestic and abroad, should stand at about 36 GW at that time. By 2020, if current growth trends are sustained, over 150,000 Americans will be employed in the PV industry.

Environmentally Friendly

PV's ability to generate electricity while producing no atmospheric emissions or greenhouse gases marks it as a technology of choice. A 2.5 kW system (enough to power a typical home) covers less than 400 square feet of rooftop. Over the course of a year, it saves about the same amount of carbon dioxide that a car emits during that period.

The public recognizes, now more than ever, that it is time to embrace renewable technologies. A recent *Newsweek* poll recorded that 84 percent of Americans desire more federal investment in solar and wind energy. In November 2001, 73 percent of voters in San Francisco supported a $100 million bond to place solar on buildings in their city. The Sacramento Municipal Utility Disrict (SMUD) has a waiting list of people who wish to install solar on their rooftops and has placed over 10 MW of systems in service. Home builders are partnering with companies in making solar a standard feature. In certain locations in California, Home Depot is selling complete solar energy systems. This demand will spread. Building-integrated PV systems are also gaining momentum.

Zero Net Energy Buildings

The Department of Energy's Office of Energy Efficiency and Renewable Energy, under the capable leadership of David Garman, is embarking on an initiative called zero net energy buildings (ZEB). As its name implies, the program's goal is to produce buildings that on net consume no energy. The zero net energy building will incorporate various technologies, including photovoltaics and solar thermal, to produce the home of the future. To help win the trust of the public, the federal government could play an important role by selecting certain government construction projects to be designated as zero net energy buildings.

The math shows that many small solar generating systems distributed throughout a power grid reduce the need for traditional power facilities. Don Osborn, the superintendent of renewable generation of SMUD, uses the following statistic: If every new home in California placed a 2.2 kW PV system on its rooftop, the equivalent of a 500 MW power plant would be displaced.

The shift to ZEB will benefit far more than the solar industry. Consumers will receive lower electricity bills and enjoy a cleaner environment. A more distributed electricity system will make us less vulnerable to terrorist attacks and benign disruptions. Stress on the transmission grid will be relieved. Energy independence could be achieved.

Even with a more distributed electricity model, central power stations are not likely to disappear. Rather, over time, the central energy sources should become cleaner. Among these, CSP technologies have a bright future. Congress has requested that the administration prepare a report on how to produce 1,000 MW of CSP in the Southwest. . . .

The United States boasts some of the best solar resources on earth and a people dedicated to a cleaner, more sustainable future for their children and grandchildren. If we match this boast with the groundbreaking achievements in solar energy lying within our grasp, the twenty-first century can enter the annals as the solar century.

"Solar energy . . . is simply too weak a source and far too intermittent and unreliable to be useful."

Solar Energy Is an Impractical Energy Source

Michael Fox

According to science writer and speaker Michael Fox in the following article, solar power is being promoted as a net producer of energy when in fact it is an unprofitable net consumer of energy and should not be seriously pursued as an alternative energy source. Fox cites scientific evidence showing that even if solar, or photovoltaic, cells could be produced for free, the costs of financing, installation, repair, maintenance, and replacement exceed the value of the electricity they can produce. Michael Fox holds a PhD in chemistry from the University of Washington.

As you read, consider the following questions:

1. What projects does Fox point to as proof that solar power costs more to produce than it is worth?

2. How much electricity at most can a PV cell be expected to produce, and how much work can that current do, according to Fox?

Michael Fox, "The False Promises of Solar Energy," *Hawaii Reporter*, November 30, 2005. Copyright © 2005 Hawaii Reporter, Inc. Reproduced by permission.

3. How much more costly is solar power than either wind energy or nuclear energy, according to the author?

Someone once said that "Anything is possible if you don't know what you are talking about." Discussions of energy in general and several types of "alternative energy" in particular are filled with the lack of the basics of energy. Throw in concepts of energy density and "dispatchability" and it gets more complicated.

The Laws of Thermodynamics, of Heat Transfer, and the equations for both kinetic and potential energy apply to most discussions of energy and impose immutable constraints on all energy supply systems.

These laws are typically studied in physics, chemistry, chemical engineering and other demanding classes in undergraduate and graduate schools. Entire textbooks and college curricula are written and conducted on various forms of energy. Those who have not endured such disciplines may not appreciate the properties of energy and how it is generated, transferred, and used.

One of many units of energy is the "kilowatt-hr." Although all energy units can be converted to any other, the kilowatt-hr is most often used to describe electrical energy. To get a feel for how much energy is in a kilowatt-hr, consider one of those bicycle generators used to power a light bulb (often found in museums). A very fit cyclist can keep a 100 watt light bulb lighted for an hour. If he can do this for 10 hours he will deliver 1000 watt-hrs, or 1.0 kilowatt-hr (kw-hr). This is in human terms a lot of effort.

Now consider a 1000 megawatt (MW) power plant (the megawatt is a unit of power, not energy). In the same 10 hours for the cyclist above, this power plant can deliver 10 × 1000 × 1,000,000 = 10 billion watt-hrs or 10 million kilowatt-hrs. In other words this single power plant can deliver the same amount of electrical energy as 10,000,000 cyclists. The owner of the power plant will sell each kw-hr for about 8 cents. Would those cyclists work for 8 cents for a 10 hr workday? Not likely. The waste disposal costs would be significant!

Ever since the [Jimmy] Carter Administration [1976–1980], the U.S. government has spent billions on solar energy research, development, and demonstrations. Thousands of demonstrations have been constructed across the United States. Whether it's the Solar One Power Tower in the California desert or the Luz project there also, or the hundreds across the U.S. I am not aware of any successes. The exceptions might be for water heating (not electricity) in the southern latitudes. Most have been dismal engineering failures. Before spending billions more, this nation would do well to revisit these past projects to learn what went wrong. Such learning is precisely why we built these projects in the first place, so let's learn!

Solar Power Is Not Cost-Effective

We learned for example that the heavily subsidized Solar Power Tower in Southern Cal. before it caught fire could not provide on an annual basis enough electricity for its own on-site use, lights, air conditioning, computers, etc. On an annual basis it was a net energy consumer, not a true source!

In Eastern Washington as in other states there were many such lesser projects. A Washington congressman in the early 80s was Mike McCormick, who was among the first to sponsor legislation for these solar projects. There were a number of such projects built there. Across the nation many billions of government funds were passed out for the demonstrations. So far as can be determined none were successful from either a performance or cost perspective. A radically designed bank building in Richland, Washington, still exists where one of the projects was undertaken in the 80s. The intentions were to provide solar energy to heat the building with heated circulating water. The maintenance costs were prohibitive and the engineering performance was a failure. The system has been closed down for years. Today one can still see the burst circulation lines, the corrosion, not to mention bird droppings and dust deposits on the collectors. Such maintenance costs are routinely overlooked in cost analyses and projections.

Another half-million-dollar project was installed on the top of a one-story office building. It too was a stunning failure because of high maintenance requirements, but nevertheless cost the taxpayers more than $500,000. The working fluid was ethylene glycol (antifreeze). When the system sprang a leak many cars in the parking lot were sprayed with the chemical, ruining the paint jobs of many of them. Such building owners are eager to accept such massive funds, the public relations coup, as well as the politically correct accolades for "alternative energy" efforts. The romance disappears when the maintenance and repairs costs roll in year after year. It too was shut down because of these unrelenting costs.

As with bad marriages these projects became eyesores and never worked. Removal of the failed solar collectors was a requirement for the sale of the property. The history of the U.S. solar energy program over the past 30 years has been a long string of broken promises and the waste of billions [of dollars]. The simplistic assertions and empty promises continue today as if we haven't learned a thing from the billions spent already. I can provide a tour of failed solar projects if desired, which litter the area, as well as failed windmills added as a bonus. The costs and performance of solar electric projects are even worse. The amount of solar energy striking a collector depends upon several factors including the distance from the sun and the latitude north or south of the equator. According to retired physicist Howard Hayden, at the latitude of Hartford, Connecticut, the incoming solar energy (called insolation) averages 160 watts/sq meter. This is a fixed upper value for this latitude. . . .

Solar Power Costs Too Much

According to the Cato Institute, solar generating capacity represents 0.05% of U.S. total capacity and in 1995 actually produced 0.03% of electricity. Solar-power capacity is triple the cost of new gas-generated electricity and quadruple the cost of surplus power.

The Cato report says, "A 1978 study found that the materials required for thermal-solar projects were 1,000 times greater than for a similarly sized fossil-fuel facility, creating substantial incremental energy consumption and industrial pollution. A major environmental cost of photovoltaic solar energy is toxic chemical pollution (arsenic, gallium, and cadmium) and energy consumption associated with the large-scale manufacture of photovoltaic panels. The installation phase has distinct environmental consequences, given the large land masses required for such solar farms—some 5 to 10 acres per MW of installed capacity." A gas-fired plant needs about 1/3 of an acre per megawatt.

Jonathan DuHamel, "The False Promise of 'Renewable' Energy," People for the USA, September 2004. www.people4theusa.org.

Values Drop When the Sun Is Not Out

In fact the average insolation in 2/3 of the United States is within 20% of this value. . . . Although this is an upper limit, there is a huge daily drop-off in this value, which includes zero power every night! The need for an equally sized non-solar backup [electrical] system for night time and cloudy days [is] obvious.

The 160 w/sq m value is only the thermal (heat) energy flux at noon on a sunny day. To convert this to electrical energy, photovoltaic (PV) cells are required. This gets very expensive. The cells are typically 10% efficient. In other words from that 160 watt/sq meter thermal power, we can expect about 16 watts/sq meter of electric power! This is not enough to operate a single refrigerator light! Furthermore, the electricity from the PV cells are direct current and low voltage. To make this electricity useful it needs more electrical equipment to convert it to alternating current at higher voltages such as 110 volts AC [alternating current]. This also adds to the costs.

An engineering friend in Sacramento [California] was researching solar photovoltaic electricity for installation on his home there. He contacted Sacramento Municipal Utility District (SMUD) to discuss the design and costs. He was told that for a 1500 watt photovoltaic (PV) system placed on his roof it would cost $14,000 to $16,000! Being surprised at this huge cost he asked the intelligent question, "Does that include a storage system (batteries, controls, and distribution systems to supply electrical energy at night)?" He was told that it didn't and that the storage system would cost an additional $30,000!

Too often alternative energy advocates throw solar and wind energy into the discussions as if these were the sources of all our future energy needs. Nothing could be further from the truth and it's dangerous for our leaders to believe so.

The American Physical Society concluded in 1979 that even if the PV cells were *free* the other costs would still make solar electricity's cost prohibitive. University of Arizona physicists and solar energy experts Drs. Aden and Marjorie Meinel said essentially the same thing in their Congressional testimony in the early 80s. Their testimony addressed solar space heating, water pumping, and solar voltaics. Hot water heating may be near-economical at the lower latitudes but not in the upper 2/3 of the US. The Meinels pointed out these hidden costs to include financing, installation, repair, maintenance, and replacement.

Nuclear Costs Less than Solar

In the planning for their future energy choices Japan and Switzerland performed energy cost comparisons. Both nations found nominally the same cost disparities in wind, solar, and nuclear. In comparing costs of nuclear energy with both solar and wind energy costs, these nations independently found that solar electricity was a nominal 30 times more costly and wind energy 3 times the costs of nuclear energy. This helps explain why so many nations are building large nuclear programs and not wind or solar facilities. China for example is currently building 8 reactors and has 20 more in the design stages. They are also building huge hydro facilities and a large number of coal plants.

It hasn't been widely noticed but the same movement which opposes serious oil exploration and drilling, coal burning, nuclear energy, natural gas in places, are also involved with the promotion of the failed solar and wind technologies. Those former sources collectively produce more than 98% of the nation's electricity. Electrical energy is essential to any advanced nation. Destroying 98% of the electrical energy generating systems would turn the United States into another Third World country. Their actions do not match their words on many levels. The promise of solar energy has been shown to fail. It is simply too weak a source and far too intermittent and unreliable to be useful.

> *"Wind energy is zero-emissions energy, a renewable resource that is one of our last, best hopes for staving off devastating climate change."*

Wind Power Should Be Pursued

Jim Motavalli

In the following viewpoint, Jim Motavalli promotes the development of wind power in the United States, which presently gets less than 1 percent of its energy from wind power. He argues that the expansion of wind power, fostered by federal tax credits, could offset a projected natural gas supply shortage of 3 to 4 billion cubic feet per day. Motavalli supports offshore wind farms in particular, and describes the proposed Cape Wind farm project off Cape Cod, Massachusetts, as a potentially beneficial installation. Jim Motavalli is the editor of E: The Environmental Magazine, *a nonpartisan bimonthly publication on environmental issues.*

As you read, consider the following questions:

1. According to the author, how much of the energy in Germany and Denmark is supplied by wind power?

Jim Motavalli, "Catching the Wind," *E Magazine*, January-February, 2005, pp. 26–39. Copyright © 2005. Reproduced with permission from E/The Environmental Magazine.

2. What RPS figure does Motavalli say Congress should mandate by 2020?

3. According to Bill McKibben, quoted by Motavalli, what fact should override opposition to the Cape Wind project?

At the base of the Sagamore Bridge, the gateway to Cape Cod, is a nostalgia-inducing fake windmill that looks like it belongs with tulips and wooden shoes in an image of Holland's colorful past. In fact, it's advertising for a Christmas tree store, but its mere presence is an irony as the Cape is convulsed in an epic battle over some very real wind turbines. Cape Wind plans to build the first offshore wind park in the U.S. in Nantucket Sound, just five miles off the coast of some of the most exclusive real estate in America. If the project is built, it will at least temporarily set a record as the largest wind farm in the world, its 130 turbines producing 420 megawatts of electricity. If it is defeated by a well-funded opposition group with some highly placed political allies, it will be a resounding defeat for wind power in the U.S., but possibly just a minor setback for a worldwide renewable energy movement that is filling its sails with the inexhaustible power of the wind.

The Growing Power of Wind

Even as the world experiences ever-more-severe storms and sets new temperature records that are being linked to global warming, we're also setting new records for installed wind energy. The two phenomena might appear to be unrelated, but actually they're closely tied together. Wind energy is zero-emissions energy, a renewable resource that is one of our last, best hopes for staving off devastating climate change. Wind energy has grown 28 percent annually [since 2000], and the so-called "installed capacity" (the generating power of working wind turbines) doubles every three years: It is the fastest-growing energy source in the world. Some 6,000 megawatts of wind capacity—enough to power 1.5 million homes—are added annually.

The old-fashioned windmills that once pumped water for local farmers have been replaced with high-technology, high-efficiency industrial-grade turbines. The General Electric [GE] turbines scheduled to be installed by Cape Wind (resulting from GE's purchase of Enron's wind assets at fire-sale prices) offer a whopping 3.6 megawatts each, are 40 stories tall on thin towers, and boast three prop-like blades the length of two jumbo jets.

As *Business 2.0* reports, "Since 1985, the electric generating capacity of a typical windmill has gone from about 100 kilowatts of constant power to 1.5 megawatts, with a corresponding reduction in cost from 12 cents per kilowatt-hour to less than five cents." Because of federal tax credits (renewed until the end of 200[7]) the real cost of wind power is getting close to such perennials as nuclear, coal and natural gas, which explains the interest of big profit-oriented companies like GE. In 2001, 6,500 megawatts of new wind-generating capacity were installed worldwide, and by 2003 the world had 39,000 megawatts of installed wind power. . . .

A Bright Future . . . with Clouds

The U.S. . . . and Europe dominate the development and installation of wind power. Large-scale wind farms, both on- and off-shore, can now be found from Denmark to New Zealand. Europe has more than 28,000 installed megawatts of wind power (70 percent of world capacity). World wind leaders include Germany, the U.S., Spain, Denmark and India, each with more than 2,000 megawatts. Germany is in the lead, with 14,609 megawatts installed by the end of 2003. The wind energy industry in Germany employs 35,000 people and supplies 3.5 percent of the nation's electricity. Denmark has the world's highest proportion of electricity generated by wind, more than 20 percent. The Danish Wind Energy Association would like to see that ratcheted up to 35 percent wind power by 2015.

U.S. Wind Industry Rebounds

In the U.S. (which gets less than one percent of its energy from wind) the industry rebounded somewhat in the late 1990s. There are now clusters of wind turbines in Texas and Colorado, as well as newly updated sites in California. According to the American Wind Energy Association (AWEA), there are now wind energy products in almost every state west of the Mississippi, and in many Northeastern states. California leads with more than 2,042 megawatts of installed wind energy, followed by Texas, which experienced 500 percent wind growth in 2001 and now has 1,293 megawatts. AWEA explains that one megawatt of wind capacity is enough to supply 240 to 300 average American homes, and California's wind power alone can save the energy equivalent of 4.8 million barrels of oil per year.

AWEA says the U.S. wind industry will install up to 3,000 megawatts of new capacity by 2009. If that proves true, the U.S. will have nearly 10,000 megawatts of wind power, enough to power three million homes. The economics of wind are looking increasingly good. The cost of generating a kilowatt-hour of electricity from wind power has dropped from $1 in 1978 to five cents in 1998, and is expected to drop even further, to 2.5 cents. Wind turbines themselves have dropped in installed cost to $800 per kilowatt. Although, according to the *Financial Times*, wind power is still twice as expensive as generation from a modern oil-fired plant, federal subsidies and tax benefits available in many countries level the playing field.

One of the biggest hindrances to even greater wind installation in the U.S. is the on-again, off-again nature of the federal wind energy production tax credit (PTC). Introduced as part of the Energy Policy Act of 1992, PTC granted 1.5 cents per kilowatt-hour (since adjusted for inflation) for the first 10 years of operation to wind plants brought on line before the end of June 1999. A succession of short-term renewals and expirations of PTC led to three boom-and-bust cycles (the most recent a boom in 2003 and a bust in 2004) in wind power installation. Its current extension to the end of 2005 may see some wind projects struggling to meet the PTC requirements before the credit expires once again.

Sustainable Energy Standard

The U.S. could go further, and states with big wind resources would reap major rewards. If Congress were to establish a 20 percent national renewable energy standard by 2020 (requiring utilities to sell a fifth of their energy from sustainable sources), the Union of Concerned Scientists reports, wind-rich North Dakota could gain $1.4 billion in new investment from wind and other renewables. North Dakota consumers would save $363 million in lower electricity bills annually if the standard were combined with improvements in energy efficiency. The environment would also benefit with a 28 percent reduction in carbon dioxide emissions from the plains states. A watered-down version of this "renewables portfolio standard" (RPS) was included in the 2002 and 2003 versions of the failed federal energy bill, but failed to make the final cut.

Just such an RPS, on the state level, was enacted when George W. Bush was governor of Texas, and led that state to its pre-eminent status as the number two wind generator in the U.S. Governor George Pataki issued an executive order establishing such an RPS for New York State: 20 percent renewables by 2010. New York currently gets 17 percent of its electricity from renewable sources, principally hydro power. The 2004 elections may have been terrible news for the environment, but one bright spot was the passage of a Colorado RPS that will require the state to buy 10 percent of its energy from renewable sources by 2015. Seventeen states have now enacted RPS rules.

The Benefits of the Cape Wind Project

If built, the Cape Wind project will contribute significantly to addressing many of the major problems our current electricity system poses. The . . . findings on socioeconomic impacts include $1.5–2 billion in economic benefits to the U.S. economy, New England consumer savings on electricity bills of $25 million per year during the first five years of operation ($10 million for Massachusetts consumers), decreased costs associated with adverse health impacts from fossil fuel plants of $53 million per year, and almost 400 full-time new jobs created directly or indirectly due to the project.

Union of Concerned Scientists, "Comments on the Cape Wind Draft Environmental Impact Statement." www.ucsusa.org.

AWEA thinks that, with a favorable political climate, the U.S. could have 100,000 megawatts of installed wind power by 2013, with a full potential of 600,000 megawatts. The group points out that wind power could offset a projected three to four billion cubic feet per day natural gas supply shortage in the U.S.

Even in the absence of a lucrative production tax credit, wind projects are moving forward. Current projects include construction of the world's third-largest wind farm, with 136 turbines and 204 megawatts capacity, in New Mexico as part of the utility-run New Mexico Wind Energy Center. FPL Energy is also installing 162 megawatts of 1.8-megawatt Danish-made Vestas turbines in Solano County, California for the High Winds project. New England can boast of Green Mountain Power's project in Searsburg, Vermont, which was completed in 1997 and features 11 turbines generating six megawatts.

Other projects are underway in Oklahoma and South Dakota, on the Rosebud Sioux reservation. Tex Hall of the National Congress of American Indians observes that "tribes here [in the Great Plains] have many thousands of megawatts of potential wind power blowing across our reservation lands. . . . Tribes need access to the federal grid to bring our value-added electricity to market throughout our region and beyond."

Local Opposition to Offshore Farms

Many of the largest wind farms today are being built offshore, with varying amounts of controversy. Despite its proximity to Jones Beach, one of the largest summer recreational destinations in the New York area (with six million annual visitors), the proposed Long Island Offshore Wind Initiative (with between 25 and 50 turbines, producing up to four megawatts each) has not generated significant opposition, although it could develop as plans move forward. The Long Island wind farm "will be pollution-free, boundless and blow a gust of clean air into the future of energy production," says Ashok Gupta of the Natural Resources Defense Council.

With peak energy demand on Long Island soaring (up 10 percent just between 2001 and 2002), there is clearly a need for new and cleaner sources of electricity. On the western end of the South Shore, the utility-owned wind farm would be two to five miles offshore and provide electricity for 30,000 homes when completed in 2007. Long Island's suffering air would benefit from the annual reduction of 834 tons of sulfur dioxide, 332 tons of nitrogen oxide and 227,000 tons of climate-altering carbon dioxide. Taken as a whole, Long Island has incredible potential wind resources along its south shore extending past Montauk Point. According to one study, a string of wind farms in that region could produce 5,200 megawatts of power, or enough to meet 77 percent of Long Island's ever-expanding needs.

Germany is a world leader in offshore wind, and recently finalized an agreement to build a 350-megawatt project (with 70 five-megawatt turbines) off the island of Rügen. Britain's

Crown Estate, which owns the UK's territorial seabed, has granted approval for 13 offshore wind farms, and British utility Powergen has plans to develop a giant 500-megawatt offshore farm in the Thames estuary near London. The Irish government has approved a 520-megawatt wind farm offshore southeast of Dublin. China is building a 400-megawatt facility 60 miles from Beijing, and says confidently it will be generating 12 percent of its energy from renewables by 2020.

Cape Wind Project

None of these projects have met with the kind of opposition that stalks the Cape Wind project, a planned $700 million development that would cover 26 square miles off Cape Cod. That wind farm, with General Electric turbines up to 40 stories tall, would surpass Denmark's Horns Reef as the world's largest.

The proposal has split the environmental community, drawing opposition from such powerful environmental allies as Robert Kennedy Jr. "I'm a strong advocate of wind farms on the oceans and high seas," says Kennedy. "But there are appropriate places for everything. We wouldn't put one of these in Yosemite, and I think environmentalists are falling into a trap if they think the only wilderness areas worth preserving are in the Rocky Mountains or American West. The most important are the ones close to our cities, where the public has access to them. And Nantucket Sound is a wilderness, which people need to experience. I always get nervous when people talk about privatizing the commons. In this case, the benefits of the power extracted from Nantucket Sound are far outweighed by the other values that our communities derive from it."

Writer Bill McKibben, however, argues in *Orion* that the criticisms amount to "small truths." The bigger point is that Nantucket's air contains 370 parts per million of carbon dioxide, up from 275 parts per million before the Industrial Revolution. "And if we keep burning coal and gas and oil, the scientific consensus is that by the latter part of the century the planet's temperature will have risen five degrees Fahrenheit to a level higher than we've seen for 50 million years." The choice, he writes, "is not between windmills and untouched nature, it's between windmills and the destruction of the planet's biology on a scale we can barely begin to imagine."

> *"Windfarms ... produce no useful electricity and make no reduction to emissions from power generation."*

The Drawbacks of Wind Power Far Outweigh the Benefits

Eric Rosenbloom

The following viewpoint disputes wind-power advocates' claims that wind turbine installations are an efficient, low-cost alternative energy source. Author Eric Rosenbloom maintains that, on the contrary, wind power does nothing to reduce emissions from or displace fossil-fuel burning energy plants, degrades rural and wild areas, and is unreliable because its output fluctuates so much. He cites studies from the United Kingdom, Germany, Vermont, and Denmark that all admit wind power's significant drawbacks outweigh its theoretical benefits. Eric Rosenbloom is a freelance writer and science editor living in Vermont.

As you read, consider the following questions:

1. According to the British Royal Academy of Engineering study cited by Rosenbloom, what is the difference between the hypothetical national wind-power output and the actual, measured wind-power output?

Eric Rosenbloom, "The Low Benefit of Industrial Wind," *American Wind Energy Opposition*, January 20, 2006. Reproduced by permission.

2. Why must wind-power construction be accompanied by nearly equal conventional power-plant construction, according to the author?

3. Why does Rosenbloom say utility companies want to be part of wind-power development?

Driving the desire for industrial wind power is the conviction that it will help reduce fossil and/or nuclear fuel use. Thus the local impacts of large wind turbine installations—with their clearing of trees, substantial concrete foundations, new roads, transmission support, flashing lights, and grinding noise—are thought to be justified by a greater good of healthier air and water, reduction of carbon emissions, and moving away from harmful mining and fuel wars. These are all without question important goals.

While the wind power industry tends to downplay its negative effects, many conservation groups call for careful siting and ongoing study to minimize them. There is debate, therefore, about the impacts but not about the benefits. Even the most cautious of advocates do not doubt, for example, that "every kilowatt-hour generated by wind is a kilowatt-hour not generated by a dirty fuel."

That may be true for a small home turbine with substantial battery storage, but such a formula is, at best, overly simplistic for large turbines meant to supply the grid. The evidence from countries that already have a large proportion of wind power suggests that it has very little, if any, effect on the use of other sources. This is not surprising when one learns how the grid works: A rise in wind power most likely just causes a thermal plant to switch from generation to standby, in which mode it continues to burn fuel.

Studies Demonstrate the Limitations of Wind Power

1. "Impact of Wind Power Generation in Ireland on the Operation of Conventional Plant and the Economic Implica-

Wind Power Is Hot Air

Windfarms are far from environmentally benign. If you think a conventional power plant occupying 20 acres is an eyesore, think about this: In a January 2000 article in *Foreign Affairs*, Richard Rhodes and Denis Beller estimate that a 1,000-megawatt windfarm (equivalent to a medium-sized conventional power plant) would occupy 2,000 square miles. That means replacing the 604,000 megawatts of total generating capacity in the United States with windmills would occupy 1.2 million square miles, a third of the country's total land area. And even that wouldn't really work, since windmills typically produce only a third of their rated capacity because the wind doesn't always blow.

Ronald Bailey, Reason, *July 10, 2002.*

tions," ESB National Grid, February 2004. This study by the Irish grid manager finds that the benefits of wind-generated power are small and that they decrease as more wind power is added to the system. Their model generously assumes that all energy produced from wind facilities would be used and did not consider output fluctuations within time periods of less than an hour.

They describe three problems that mitigate the benefits of wind power:

- large amount of extra energy required to start up thermal generators that would otherwise not have been turned off

- mechanical stresses of more frequent ramping of production levels up and down

- increased prices of energy necessary to pay for any lower usage of thermal plants.

Wind plants add more capacity (requiring more infrastructure) with almost no reduction of non-wind capacity, the latter of which must be used more inefficiently than otherwise. As for CO_2 [carbon dioxide] reduction, the study concludes,

> The cost of CO_2 abatement arising from using large levels of wind energy penetration appears high relative to other alternatives.

Their model generously assumes that all energy produced from wind facilities is used and disregards output fluctuations within time periods of less than an hour. And they did not consider at all the environmental toll of expanded industrial wind development.

2. "Response to the House of Lords Science and Technology Select Committee Inquiry into the Practicalities of Developing Renewable Energy," Royal Academy of Engineering [U.K.], October 2003. This report shows that even with generous assumptions of wind power performance, as its share of generating capacity increases, its ability to displace conventional sources decreases—the conclusion also reached by EirGrid (preceding) and E.ON Netz (following). To meet the U.K.s peak of 50,000 MW for 90 of 100 winters, 59,000 MW of conventional capacity is currently maintained along with 500 MW of wind plant. If the amount of wind is increased to the 2010 target of 7,500 MW, 57,000 MW of conventional capacity must still be kept. With the 2020 target of 25,000 MW of wind, conventional capacity is still at 55,000 MW. That is, wind power is essentially adding surplus capacity rather than replacing conventional plants.

> From wind data records covering the whole of mainland UK, there is a sizeable probability of little or no wind blowing across the entire country, regardless of the capacity installed. Figure 1 illustrates the situation where a hypothetical

wind power capacity of 7,300 MW installed throughout the country is correlated with actual Met Office wind data. The most likely power output nationally is seen to be less than 200 MW.

The report shows that one-third of the time, widespread wind power facilities in the U.K. (which boasts the best wind resource in Europe) would be producing at less than 14% of capacity. They would be producing at less than 8% capacity a fourth of the time and at 4% or less for 11% of the time.

3. "Green Mountain Power Wind Power Project Third-Year Operating Experience: 1999–2000," U.S. Department of Energy-Electric Power Research Institute [EPRI] Wind Turbine Verification Program, December 2002. EPRI reported that the ridgeline facility in Searsburg, Vermont, produced no electricity at all—not even a trickle—almost 40% of the time:

> On average, the Searsburg turbines generate electricity more than 60% of the time. . . . Individual turbines generated electricity 51% to 75% of the time during the third year, and from 45% to 77% of the time during the second year. The turbine generation time is related to both wind speed and availability.

4. "Wind Report 2005," E.ON Netz. E.ON Netz manages the transmission grid in Schleswig-Holstein and Lower Saxony, about a third of Germany, hosting 7,050 MW of Germany's 16,394 MW installed wind-generating capacity at the end of 2004. The total production in their system was 11.3 tW-h [terawatt-hours] in 2004, representing an average feed of 1,295 MW (18.3% of capacity).

> Wind energy is only able to replace traditional power stations to a limited extent. Their dependence on the prevailing wind conditions means that wind power has a limited load factor even when technically available. It is not possible to guarantee its use for the continual cover of electricity con-

sumption. Consequently, traditional power stations with capacities equal to 90% of the installed wind power capacity [a little over the maximum historical wind power infeed] must be permanently online in order to guarantee power supply at all times.

Graphs in this report (and the similar 2004 report) show that half of the time, wind power infeed is less than two-thirds of its annual average. It is greater than its annual average only a third of the time. A similar power vs. time curve applies to all wind power facilities, whether their annual average output in relation to rated capacity is higher or lower than those in Germany. The 11-turbine facility in Searsburg, Vermont, produces no power at all more than a third of the time.

Both cold wintry periods and periods of summer heat are attributable to stable high-pressure weather systems. Low wind levels are meteorologically symptomatic of such high pressure weather systems. This means that in these periods, the contribution made by wind energy to meeting electricity consumption demand is correspondingly low. . . .

The feed-in capacity can change frequently within a few hours. This is shown in the Christmas week from 20 to 26 December 2004. Whilst wind power feed-in at 9.15 am on Christmas Eve reached its maximum for the year at 6,024 MW, it fell to below 2,000 MW within only 10 hours, a difference of over 4,000 MW. This corresponds to the capacity of 8 × 500 MW coal fired power station blocks. On Boxing Day [December 26], wind power feed-in in the E.ON grid fell to below 40 MW. . . .

In 2004 two major German studies investigated the size of contribution that wind farms make towards guaranteed capacity. Both studies separately came to virtually identical conclusions, that wind energy currently contributes to the secure production capacity of the system, by providing 8% of its installed capacity.

As wind power capacity rises, the lower availability of the wind farms determines the reliability of the system as a whole to an ever increasing extent. Consequently the greater reliability of traditional power stations becomes increasingly eclipsed. As a result, the relative contribution of wind power to the guaranteed capacity of our supply system up to the year 2020 will fall continuously to around 4%. In concrete terms, this means that in 2020, with a forecast wind power capacity of over 48,000 MW, 2,000 MW of traditional power production can be replaced by these wind farms. . . .

[[T]he increased use of wind power in Germany has resulted in uncontrollable fluctuations occurring on the generation side due to the random character of wind power feed-in. This significantly increases the demands placed on the control balancing process [and bringing about rising grid costs. The massive increase in the construction of new wind power plants in recent years has greatly increased the need for wind-related reserve capacity.—*Wind Report 2004*].

That is, wind power construction must be accompanied by almost equal construction of new conventional power plants, which will be used very nearly as much as if the wind turbines were not there.

5. "Danish Wind: Too Good to Be True?" David J. White, The Utilities Journal, July 2004.

Denmark has installed 3,100 MW of wind turbine capacity to date, which is in theory capable of generating 20% of the country's electricity demand. Of that capacity, 2,374 MW is located in western Denmark (Jutland and Funen). The statistic is misleading because it implies that 20% of Denmark's power is supplied continuously from its wind capacity, but the figure appears to be a promotional statistic rather than a factual representation of the supply pattern.

Jutland has cable connections to Norway, Sweden and Germany with a capacity of 2,750 MW. In other words, it has the means of exporting all of its wind production. The 2003 annual report of Eltra, the western Denmark transmission company, suggests an export figure of 84% of total wind production to these countries in 2003, with figures that ramped up rapidly over previous years as Denmark found that it could not absorb wind output into the domestic system.

There is no CO_2 saving in Danish exchange with Norway and Sweden because wind power only displaces CO_2-free generated power. When the power is consumed in Denmark itself, fluctuations in wind output have to be managed by the operation of fossil-fired capacity below optimum efficiency in order to stabilise the grid (i.e., spinning reserve). Elsam, the Jutland power generator, stated ... at a meeting of the Danish Wind Energy Association with the Danish government that increasing wind power does not decrease CO_2 emissions. Ireland has drawn similar conclusions based on its experience that *the rate of change of wind speed can drop faster than the rate at which fossil-fuelled capacity can be started up* [emphasis added]. Hence spinning reserve is essential, although it leads to a minimal CO_2 saving on the system. Innogy made the same observation about the operation of the UK system [D. Tolley, presentation to Institute of Mechanical Engineers, January 2003].

The result is that, while wind-generated power itself is CO_2-free, the saving to the whole power system is not proportional to the amount of fossil-fuelled power that it displaces. The operation of fossil-fired capacity as spinning reserve emits more CO_2/kWh than if the use of that plant were optimised, thus offsetting much of the benefit of wind.

6. Flemming Nissen, head of development, Elsam (operating 404 MW of wind power in Denmark), presentation to "Vind eller forsvind" conference, Copenhagen, May 27, 2004.

Increased development of wind turbines does not reduce Danish CO_2 emissions.

7. *"Windfarms provide no useful electricity," Richard S. Courtney, presentation to conference of Groups Opposed to Windfarms in the UK, 2004.*

Electricity is wanted all the time but the demand for electricity varies from hour to hour, day to day, and month to month. The electricity grid has to match the supply of electricity to the demand for it at all times. This is difficult because power stations cannot be switched on and off as demand varies [because they take so long—several hours to a couple of days—to warm up].

The problem of matching electricity supply to varying demand is overcome by operating power stations in three modes called "base load," "generation," and "spinning standby."

Some power stations operate all the time providing electricity to the grid, and they are said to provide "base load."

Other power stations also operate all the time but do not provide electricity all the time. They burn (or fission) their fuel to boil water and superheat the resulting steam which is fed to the steam turbines that are thus kept hot and spinning all the time. Of course, they emit all the emissions from use of their fuel all the time. But some of this time they dump heat from their cooling towers instead of generating electricity, and they are then said to be operating "spinning standby."

One or more power stations can be instantly switched from spinning standby to provide electricity to match an increase to demand for electricity. It is said to be operating 'generation' when it is providing electricity. Power stations are switched between spinning standby and generation as demand for electricity changes. . . .

Windfarms only provide electricity when the wind is strong enough and not too strong. As they suddenly provide electricity when the wind changes, the grid operator must match this changed supply of electricity to the existing demand for electricity. This is achieved by switching a power station to spinning standby mode. That power station continues to operate in this mode so it can provide electricity when the windfarm stops supplying electricity because the wind has changed again.

Windfarms only force power stations to operate more spinning standby. They provide no useful electricity and make no reduction to emissions from power generation. Indeed, the windfarm is the *cause* of emissions from a power station operating spinning standby in support of the windfarm.

Summary

The addition of industrial wind power, which is nondispatchable and varies according to the wind, requires corresponding maintenance and eventually addition of back-up conventional power, along with expansion of transmission capacity.

The accommodation of wind power causes thermal plants to run less efficiently, adding to financial costs and increasing emissions.

Spinning standby power must be kept burning to cover the short-term fluctuations of wind power. Thus, while wind power may displace generation of power from such plants, it does not displace the burning of fuel in them—the heat is simply diverted.

The most glaring cost of big wind is industrial development of rural and wild areas, which inarguably degrades rather than improves our common environment. That is impossible to justify if the benefits claimed by the industry's sales material are in fact an illusion, propped up by subsidies and artificial markets for "indulgence credits" which allow the flouting of emissions caps and renewable energy targets.

Why then do utilities generally support wind as a renewable power source? Actually, they don't. In Japan, as reported by Asahi *Shinbun* on May 18, 2005, utilities severely limit the amount of wind power on their systems, because, as documented above, "introducing too much of the electricity, whose supply can fluctuate wildly, can cause problems for utilities' power grids. . . . If there is no wind, the utilities must rely entirely on other facilities. And even when wind power can satisfy all of the demand, they must continue operating thermal generators to be ready for any abrupt shortfalls in wind power." With so-called market solutions such as renewable portfolio standards (RPS), utilities must buy a specified proportion of their power from renewable sources or buy credits equal to their shortfall. As long as they can say that, for example, 20% of their power comes from wind, it doesn't matter if they're burning as much nonrenewable fuel as ever to back it up. Most importantly, however, "green credits" are generated in addition to actual electricity. They are tokens of the renewable energy already sold but are much more valuable. Burdened with the directive to buy renewable energy, utilities want to be a part of wind power development so they can share in the lucrative sale of the credits. Ironically, analyses for New Jersey utilities and by the U.S. Energy Information Agency have shown that the only effect on emissions that an RPS might have is to drive down the cost of exceeding emissions caps or missing renewables targets.

With rising fuel prices, however, many utilities have started to demand actual useful energy targets from wind facilities. As *Renewable Energy Access* reported on Nov. 7, 2005, from an American Wind Energy Association financing workshop in New York City, this has worried investors. Wind turbines cannot provide base load power and are unreliable providers of peak load power; they do provide, however, the very marketable appearance of green energy, though not actual relief from other sources.

> *"There is significant potential . . . to dramatically expand the use of biomass in order to continue to reduce our reliance on fossil fuels."*

Biomass Is a Proven Renewable Resource with Many Uses

U.S. Department of Energy

The U.S. Department of Energy (DOE) Energy Efficiency and Renewable Energy Biomass Program promotes the development of technology to advance biomass—any organic matter such as wood, plants, residue from agriculture or forestry, and the organic component of municipal and industrial wastes—as a renewable energy source. The authors of the following DOE report describe the many uses of biomass, including fuel, chemical, and power production. They claim that biomass technologies are environmentally benign and can reduce the emission of nitrogen oxides, sulfur dioxide, and other fossil-fuel pollutants.

As you read, consider the following questions:

1. According to the DOE program, what two conversion technologies turn biomass into base chemicals from which an array of products can be made?

U.S. Department of Energy, "Biomass Basics," www.eere.energy.gov, January 25, 2006.

2. What is the difference between the carbon dioxide emissions released by burning fossil fuels and the carbon dioxide emissions released by burning biomass, according to the authors?
3. What are some of the products now made from petroleum that could be made from biomass, according to the authors?

Biomass includes all plant and plant-derived material—essentially all energy originally captured by photosynthesis. This means that biomass is a fully renewable resource and that its use for biomass-derived fuels, power, chemicals, materials, or other products essentially generates no net greenhouse gas. (You must consider any fossil-fuel use to grow, collect, and convert the biomass in a full life-cycle analysis, but the carbon dioxide released when biomass is burned is balanced by the carbon dioxide captured when the biomass is grown.) Its production and use will also generally be domestic, so it has substantial environmental, economic, and security benefits.

Biomass is already making key contributions today. It has surpassed hydro-electric power as the largest domestic source of renewable energy. Biomass currently supplies over 3% of the U.S. total energy consumption—mostly through industrial heat and steam production by the pulp and paper industry and electrical generation with forest industry residues and municipal solid waste (MSW). Of growing importance are biomass-derived ethanol and biodiesel which provide the only renewable alternative liquid fuel for transportation, a sector that strongly relies on imported oil.

In addition to today's uses of biomass, and historic ones for food, shelter, and clothing, there is significant potential for new biomass feedstocks to dramatically expand the use of biomass in order to continue to reduce our reliance on fossil fuels. The first feedstocks for this "new" biomass might come

Biomass Has Many Components and Many Uses

Biomass is material that comes from plants. Plants use the light energy from the sun to convert water and carbon dioxide to sugars that can be stored, through a process called photosynthesis. Organic waste is also considered to be biomass, because it began as plant matter. Researchers are studying how the sugars in the biomass can be converted to more usable forms of energy like electricity and fuels.

U.S. Dept. of Energy, "ABC's of Biofuels,"
Energy Efficiency and Renewable Energy Biomass Program,
February 8, 2006.

from opportunities with particular industrial residues, but beyond that, large-scale expansion of biomass is expected to come from forestry and agricultural residues. The latter includes cellulosic stalks, leaves, husks, and straw in addition to the starchy grains and oily seeds currently used. In the longer term, the biomass industry could support dedicated energy crops specifically grown for energy use.

Of the many possible conversion technologies for expanded biomass use, two of the most promising are the sugar platform and the thermochemical platform. These are referred to as "platforms" because the basic technology would generate base or platform chemicals from which industry could make a wide range of fuels, chemicals, materials, and power. These platform chemicals and wide range of products are analogous to the current petrochemicals industry. The promotion of "biorefineries" as a major new domestic biomass industry is, along with reducing dependence on imported oil, the major objective of the Biomass Program. . . .

Environmental Benefits

Biofuels are essentially nontoxic and biodegrade readily. Every gallon of biofuels used reduces the hazard of toxic petroleum product spills from oil tankers and pipeline leaks (average of 12 million gallons per year, more than what spilled from the *Exxon Valdez*, according to the U.S. Department of Transportation). In addition, using biofuels reduces the risk of groundwater contamination from underground gasoline storage tanks (more than 46 million gallons per year from 16,000 small oil spills, according to the General Accounting Office), and runoff of vehicle engine oil and fuel.

The U.S. transportation sector is responsible for one-third of our country's carbon dioxide (CO_2) emissions, the principal greenhouse gas contributing to global warming. Combustion of biofuels also releases CO_2, but because biofuels are made from plants that just recently captured that CO_2 from the atmosphere—rather than billions of years ago—that release is largely balanced by CO_2 uptake for the plants' growth. The CO_2 released when biomass is converted into biofuels and burned in truck or automobile engines is recaptured when new biomass is grown to produce more biofuels. Depending upon how much fossil energy is used to grow and process the biomass feedstock, this results in substantially reduced net greenhouse gas emissions. Modern, high-yield corn production is relatively energy intense, but the net greenhouse gas emission reduction from making ethanol from corn grain is still about 20%. Making biodiesel from soybeans reduces net emissions nearly 80%. Producing ethanol from cellulosic material also involves generating electricity by combusting the non-fermentable lignin. The combination of reducing both gasoline use and fossil electrical production can mean a greater than 100% net greenhouse gas emission reduction. . . .

Biobased Products

Many of the products now made from petroleum (e.g., petrochemicals) could be made from renewable biomass. The basic molecules in petrochemicals are hydrocarbons. In plant resources, the basic molecules are carbohydrates, proteins, and plant oils. Both plant and petroleum molecules can be processed to create building blocks for industry to manufacture a wide variety of consumer goods, including plastics, solvents, paints, adhesives, and drugs.

During the last century hydrocarbon feedstocks have dominated as industrial inputs. However, reserves of petroleum are finite and, while expected to last well into the next century, could be significantly depleted as the world population grows and standards of living improve in developing countries. Renewable plant resources will be one way to supplement hydrocarbon resources and meet increasing worldwide needs for consumer goods. We are currently witnessing the emergence of new biobased commercial and industrial chemicals, pharmaceuticals, and products. Utilization of these products on a larger scale has the potential to make an impact on reducing U.S. reliance on fossil fuels and sequestering carbon, both of which benefit the environment.

*"Geothermal energy has the ability to
. . . generate electricity in a manner
that produces minimal environmental
impacts and emissions."*

Geothermal Energy Is
a Promising Alternative
Energy Source

National Geothermal Collaborative

*In the following article, the National Geothermal Collaborative
describes geothermal energy—derived from the natural heat deep
within the earth—as a huge, untapped source of heat and electricity. According to the authors, its benefits include its constant
supply, nonfluctuating cost, low levels of harmful emissions, and
revenue potential for federal, state, and local governments. The
Denver-based National Geothermal Collaborative, formed in
2002, is an association of public- and private-sector stakeholders
who advocate the development of geothermal resources.*

As you read, consider the following questions:

1. How do geothermal plants' rates of operation compare
   with the operating rates of fossil fuel and nuclear power
   plants, according to the authors?

National Geothermal Collaborative, "Benefits of Geothermal Energy," www.geocollabo
rative.org, July 2004.

2. How can geothermal resources provide revenue to state and local governments, according to the National Geothermal Collaborative?

3. What examples of direct use of geothermal energy do the authors give?

The heat within the earth is a tremendous, but largely untapped, energy source. Just below the surface the temperature never deviates far from 55°F, but deeper beneath the surface, temperatures are hot enough to make hot water or steam. There are two ways to use the earth's heat: for generating electricity and for direct use applications. Only a few states are beginning to tap the true potential of geothermal resources. Geothermal energy has several benefits that state policymakers may wish to consider.

Geothermal energy has the ability to:

• provide reliable electricity at a stable price;

• help states diversify the mix of fuels they use to produce electricity;

• generate electricity in a manner that produces minimal environmental impacts and emissions;

• help states meet renewable portfolio standards;

• generate economic development opportunities, especially in rural areas;

• provide heat for agricultural, industrial and space heating applications. Geothermal energy can play an important part in a state's energy policy. In addition to identifying the benefits of geothermal energy, this brief also identifies some of the main challenges such as transmission constraints and regulatory barriers.

The Geysers, California: Successful Use of Geothermal Energy

The Geysers, a vapor-dominated hydrothermal system in northern California, has grown into the world's largest geothermal electrical development. At its peak in the late 1980s, about 2,100 megawatts of generating capacity were in operation. For comparison, 2,100 megawatts is roughly the equivalent of twice the electrical energy that can be generated by the turbines of Glen Canyon Dam, Arizona.

Wendell A. Duffield and John H. Sass,
Geothermal Energy: Clear Power from the Earth's Heat,
USGS Circular 1249, 2003.

Reliable Power at Stable Prices

One of the principal benefits of geothermal power plants is that they provide baseload power. Baseload power plants provide power all or most of the time and contrast with "peaker" plants which turn on or off as demand rises, or peaks, throughout the day. Geothermal plants contrast with other renewable energy resources like wind and solar energy that generate power intermittently. Geothermal plants in the United States are available to operate approximately 98 percent of the time. Such high percentages make them compare favorably with fossil fuel and nuclear power plants that operate between 75 and 90 percent of the time depending on the technology and age of the equipment.

Geothermal resources can provide power for many years. The Geysers geothermal field for example, which began commercial production in 1960 in Northern California, had the first domestic geothermal power plant. Nearly half a century later, the 21 power plants operating there generate power for approximately one million households in California. The key to successful long-term sustainable geothermal production lies in efficiently managing the resource. Technological advances—such as water injection, continue to be developed and allow developers to maximize resources and minimize drilling.

Using geothermal resources for power can help protect against volatile electricity prices. For any power plant, the price of the fuel used to generate power influences the price of the electricity produced; if the price of fuel is unpredictable, the price of electricity is unpredictable. Unlike traditional power plants that require fuel purchases, geothermal power plants secure their fuel supply before the plants begin operating. Since the price of geothermal resources will not change, it is possible to know what the price of electricity generated at a geothermal power plant will be over time. The price of electricity from new geothermal power plants ranges from between $0.05 per kWh and $0.08 per kWh. Once capital costs for the projects are recovered, the price of power can decrease below $0.05 per kWh. Fossil fuels have traditionally generated power for less, but the price of these fuels can suddenly increase to a level that is more expensive than geothermal electricity. For example, in early 2004 the price of natural gas was nearly three times what it was throughout the 1990s.

Renewable energy resources like geothermal can help states diversify the mix of fuels they rely on for power and protect customers from volatile electricity prices. The fuel costs for a geothermal power plant are not dependent upon volatile markets. In contrast, the price of natural gas is volatile and difficult to predict accurately. In addition, using domestic renewable resources can help states reduce the amount of fuel they import from nearby states or overseas.

Clean Electricity and Economic Development

Geothermal power plants produce only a small amount of air emissions. Compared to conventional fossil fuel plants, they emit very small amounts of carbon monoxide, particulate matter, sulfur dioxide, carbon dioxide, and typically no nitrogen oxides.

Fifteen states now have some sort of renewable portfolio standard (RPS) that requires power providers to supply a certain amount of their power from renewable resources by a specific year. In many of these states, electricity generated from geothermal resources can count toward meeting the standard.

Using geothermal resources can provide economic development opportunities for states in the form of property taxes, royalty payments and jobs. Geothermal power plants are the largest taxpayer in nearly every county where they exist. The 21 geothermal power plants at the Geysers Geothermal Field in California can generate almost 1,000 MW of electricity and have been an important source of revenue and jobs for Lake and Sonoma counties for many years. These power plants employ approximately 425 people full-time plus an additional full-time equivalent contract work force of 225. In 2003, property tax payments to the two counties totaled more than $11 million.

Another revenue stream flows from royalties that developers pay in exchange for the right to tap resources on federal, state or private lands. These are similar to severance taxes that states charge for extracting fuels or minerals. In 2003, operations at the Geysers generated a total of $6.15 million in federal royalties and $4.1 million in royalties to the State of California. Local county governments share in both the federal and state royalties.

Direct Use Applications

In addition to generating electricity, the heat in geothermal fluids can be used directly for such purposes as growing flowers, raising fish and heating buildings. There are a number of basic types of direct use applications: aquaculture, greenhouses, industrial and agricultural processes, resorts and spas, space and district heating, and cooling. Generally, direct use projects use fluids with temperatures of between 70°F and 300°F. Direct use systems in the United States currently provide approximately 600 thermal megawatts of heat, enough to heat approximately 115,000 average homes. (The power from direct use systems is measured in megawatts of heat as opposed to power plants that measure power in megawatts of electricity.) Some geothermal projects "cascade" geothermal energy by using the same resource for different purposes simultaneously such as heating and power. Cascading uses the resource more efficiently and may improve the economics of a project.

Four commercial greenhouses in southern New Mexico, which at times have employed up to 400 people, occupy more than 50 acres and use geothermal heat to grow plants. In 2002, these projects generated nearly $23 million in sales and paid more than $6 million in payroll. A large greenhouse in rural Utah that grows flowers employs between 80 and 120 people at different times throughout the year.

Main Challenges for Geothermal Energy

There are a variety of technical and regulatory challenges preventing the more widespread use of geothermal power. Leasing and siting processes can take long periods and be fraught with uncertainty. Although the cost of generating power from geothermal resources has decreased by 25 percent during the last two decades, exploration and drilling remain expensive and risky. Drilling costs alone can account for as much as one-third to one-half of the total cost of a project and wells typically cost between $1 and $5 million each. Detecting potentially productive geothermal reservoirs is difficult, with only about one in every five exploratory wells drilled confirming a valuable resource. The rate of success increases significantly once the resource has been found. Because some of the best geothermal resources are located in remote areas, tapping them may require an expansion of the power transmission system, which can also be expensive. Finally, power plants and direct use systems must be located near geothermal resources because it is not economic to transport hot water or steam over long distances.

"We can improve our energy security
through . . . expansion of alternative
fuels . . . [and] by generating more electricity from clean coal, advanced
nuclear power, and renewable resources."

Developing a Variety of
Renewables Can Best Solve
the Energy Crisis

National Economic Council

*In his 2006 State of the Union address, President George W.
Bush announced the Advanced Energy Initiative, committing the
United States to reduced reliance on petroleum-based energy
sources, especially foreign oil. In the following excerpt from the
initiative, the National Economic Council outlines what it considers necessary steps for achieving Bush's goal of cutting imports
of Mideast oil by 75 percent by 2025. It specifically calls for, and
increases federal funding for, a mix of alternative and renewable
energy technologies, including ethanol and biodiesel transportation fuels, hydrogen vehicles, nuclear power, advanced solar (PV)
materials, and wind-energy research.*

National Economic Council, "Advanced Energy Initiative," www.whitehouse.gov, February 2006.

As you read, consider the following questions:

1. What new miles-per-gallon standard must light trucks and SUVs meet in 2007, and what new incentive encourages consumers to buy hybrid vehicles, according to the authors?

2. How does the Advanced Energy Initiative promote the development of biomass fuel, according to the National Economic Council?

3. What is the role of the controversial Yucca Mountain, Nevada, nuclear waste storage facility in the authors' Advanced Energy Initiative?

A sound energy policy is . . . vital to national security and protecting the environment. We currently spend more than half a billion dollars a day on imported oil. We are increasingly concerned about the vulnerability of the electricity grid and pipeline systems to both unintentional and intentional disruptions. We are also focused on the environmental consequences of energy production, including emissions of air pollutants and greenhouse gases, primarily from the burning of coal, oil, and natural gas.

Since 2001, the [Bush] Administration has spent nearly $10 billion to develop cleaner, cheaper, and more reliable alternative energy sources. As a result, America is on the verge of breakthroughs in advanced energy technologies that could transform the way we produce and use energy. To build on this progress, the President's *Advanced Energy Initiative* provides for a 22% increase in funding for clean-energy technology research at the Department of Energy in two vital areas:

1. *Changing the way we fuel our vehicles.* We can improve our energy security through greater use of technologies that reduce oil use by improving efficiency, expansion of alternative fuels from homegrown biomass, and development of fuel cells that use hydrogen from domestic feedstocks.

2. *Changing the way we power our homes and businesses.* We can address high costs of natural gas and electricity by generating more electricity from clean coal, advanced nuclear power, and renewable resources such as solar and wind. . . .

Employing Existing Technologies

Consistent with the President's National Energy Policy and the energy bill signed into law [in 2005], the Administration has taken a number of steps to employ new technologies to improve the efficiency of our oil use and develop alternative fuels to displace oil.

- *Vehicle fuel economy.* The Administration increased CAFE [corporate average fuel economy] standards for light trucks and SUVs for the first time in a decade, raising the standard from 20.7 mpg to 22.2 mpg for the current model year 2007 vehicles. We have proposed additional increases in the fuel economy of light trucks and SUVs produced in model years 2008–2011, which would save 10 billion gallons of fuel over the lifetime of those vehicles.

- *Tax incentives for efficient vehicles.* The President proposed, and Congress enacted, tax incentives of up to $3,400 per vehicle to encourage purchase of highly efficient hybrid and clean diesel vehicles, which offer near-term potential to reduce demand for fuels made from crude oil.

- *Clean diesel regulations.* The Administration finalized rules that regulate emissions from both highway and non-road diesel engines and fuels, reducing emissions of sulfur and nitrogen oxides by more than 90%. Diesels offer 25–30% fuel efficiency advantage over current gasoline-engine technology, without the "black puff of smoke" of earlier versions.

- *Renewable ethanol and biodiesel.* The energy bill signed by the President established a renewable fuels standard to require the use of 7.5 billion gallons of ethanol and biodiesel by 2012, and extended tax benefits enabling both fuels to compete in today's market.

- *Alternative fuel facilities.* The energy bill also provides a 30% tax credit for installation of alternative fuel stations, up to a maximum of $30,000 per year. Currently only 556 public "E85" (85% ethanol) fueling stations exist in the U.S, and many more will be needed to increase the use of renewable fuels above the 10% that can be blended into conventional gasoline.

- *Hydrogen vehicles.* In his 2003 State of the Union Address, President Bush announced a $1.2 billion Hydrogen Fuel Initiative aimed at developing the technology for commercially viable hydrogen-powered fuel cells to power cars, trucks, homes, and businesses with no pollution or greenhouse gases.

The effects of these actions are already being seen in today's marketplace. For example, in 2005 sales of hybrid vehicles exceeded 200,000 for the first time ever, based in part on tax incentives for their purchase. And ethanol production capacity increased from 3.4 billion gallons in 2004 to 4.4 billion gallons today, with another 2.1 billion gallons of capacity currently under construction. . . .

Cellulosic Ethanol

Transportation fuels derived from biomass can be produced either by the conversion of sugar or starch crops to ethanol, or by conversion of soybean or other plant oils to produce biodiesel. These clean-burning fuels are currently mixed with gasoline or diesel fuel in small amounts (up to 10% for ethanol and up to 20% for biodiesel) and used in conventional vehicles to help reduce petroleum demand.

Cartoon by Scott Bateman. Copyright © MMIBateman.com. © North American Syndicate. Reproduced by permission.

The 3.4 billion gallons of ethanol blended into gasoline in 2004 amounted to about 2% by volume of all gasoline sold in the United States. Greater quantities of ethanol are expected to be used as a motor fuel in the future, in part due to two federal policies: an excise tax exemption of $0.51 per gallon of ethanol used as motor fuel, and a new requirement for at least 7.5 billion gallons of renewable fuel to be used in gasoline by 2012 (included in the recently passed Energy Policy Act).

Virtually all domestically produced ethanol currently comes from corn. However, corn and other starches and sugars are only a small fraction of biomass that can be used to make ethanol. A recent DOE/USDA [Dept. of Energy/U.S. Dept. of Agriculture] study suggests that, with aggressive technology developments, biofuels could supply some 60 billion gallons per year—30% of current U.S. gasoline consumption—in an environmentally responsible manner without affecting future food production.

To achieve greater use of "homegrown" renewable fuels, we will need advanced technologies that will allow competitively priced ethanol to be made from cellulosic biomass, such as agricultural and forestry residues, material in municipal solid waste, trees, and grasses. Advanced technology can break those cellulosic materials down into their component sugars and then ferment them to make fuel ethanol.

To help reduce the costs of producing these advanced biofuels, and ready these technologies for commercialization, the President's 2007 Budget increases DOE's biomass research funding by 65%, to a total of $150 million. The President's goal is to make cellulosic ethanol cost-competitive with corn-based ethanol by 2012, enabling greater use of this alternative fuel to help reduce future U.S. oil consumption.

Hydrogen Vehicles

In his 2003 State of the Union Address, President Bush announced a $1.2 billion Hydrogen Fuel Initiative to reverse America's growing dependence on foreign oil by developing the technology for commercially viable hydrogen-powered fuel cells to power cars, trucks, homes, and businesses with no pollution or greenhouse gases.

Through partnerships with the private sector, the Hydrogen Fuel Initiative and related FreedomCAR activities seek to make it practical and cost-effective for large numbers of Americans to use clean, hydrogen fuel-cell vehicles by 2020. Since hydrogen can be made from domestic fossil, nuclear and renewable energy resources, this will dramatically improve America's energy security by significantly reducing the need for oil, as well as help clean our air and reduce greenhouse gas emissions.

To continue our progress towards reducing oil consumption, the President's 2007 Budget increases funding for hydrogen technology research by $46 million over current levels. Under the President's FreedomCAR program, the Department of Energy is conducting research in partnership with industry to make today's hybrid-electric vehicle components more affordable. These components are also needed for tomorrow's hydrogen vehicles. Although we have made significant strides in reducing the high volume cost of a fuel cell by more than half, further innovations are necessary to make this technology cost-competitive. We also need to develop improved materials and methods that will allow for economic and effective hydrogen storage in vehicles and at refueling stations. A significant fraction of the hydrogen funding added by the President's budget will be used for basic research in materials science to address this fundamental challenge. Finally, we are working with industry to develop technology to enable safe production and delivery of hydrogen.

The promise of hydrogen technology is too great to ignore. The Department of Energy estimates that, if hydrogen reaches its full potential, the Hydrogen Fuel Initiative and FreedomCAR program could reduce our oil demand by over 11 million barrels per day by 2040—approximately the same amount of crude oil America imports today. . . .

Consistent with the President's National Energy Policy and the energy bill signed into law [in 2005], the Administration has taken a number of steps to develop alternatives to natural gas for electric power generation. . . .

The energy bill also provided several new programs to encourage investments in safe and reliable nuclear power: production tax incentives and "risk insurance" intended to cover costs of unforeseen legal or regulatory challenges to plant operation. Nuclear energy provides reliable and clean power.

Finally, the energy bill contained $3.4 billion over 10 years in tax incentives to encourage the production of electricity using renewable wind, solar, biomass, and geothermal energy sources, including the first-ever tax credit for residential solar energy systems. . . .

Nuclear Energy

Nuclear power provides slightly more than one-fifth of the electricity that we use to power our factories, office buildings, homes, and schools. Over 100 operating nuclear power plants, located at 65 sites in 31 states, constitute the second-largest source of electricity generation in the country. The plants are, on average, 24 years old and are licensed to operate for 40 years with an option to renew for an additional 20 years.

Nuclear power provides significant benefits to the Nation, in the form of cleaner air and low and stable electricity prices. Nuclear power does not emit the air pollutants and greenhouse gases that result from coal-fired and natural-gas-fired generation. Nuclear power is also domestic and provides energy security—North American uranium reserves are more than sufficient for the foreseeable future. Moreover, once constructed and paid for, nuclear power plants are relatively inexpensive to operate—1.8 cents per kilowatt-hour (kWh) of electricity generated. This is slightly below the operating costs of a coal-fired power plant and well below natural-gas-fired generation at current prices.

Nuclear power also faces significant challenges. New nuclear power plants require more up-front capital expense than other plants of similar size and must go through a lengthy regulatory process, which has not been tested since Congress adopted this process in 1992. The energy bill attempts to address these problems through a package of financial incentives (including Federal "risk insurance") intended to reduce the risk of an investment in a new nuclear plant. However, management of spent nuclear fuel remains an issue, both with respect to the risk it could be stolen or diverted for potential misuse and with respect to its ultimate disposition.

To enable a bright future for nuclear power, both in the United States and around the world, the President's 2007 Budget contains $250 million for the Global Nuclear Energy Partnership (GNEP). Under this partnership, America will work with nations like France, the United Kingdom, Japan, and Russia that have advanced civilian nuclear energy programs. Together, we will develop and deploy innovative, advanced reactors and new methods to recycle spent nuclear fuel. This will allow us to produce more energy, while dramatically reducing waste and eliminating many of the nuclear byproducts that could be used to make weapons.

As these technologies are developed, we will work with our partners to provide developing countries with small-scale reactors that would be secure, cost-effective, and able to meet their energy needs, as well as related nuclear services that would ensure that they have reliable fuel supply. In exchange, these countries would agree to use nuclear power only for electricity—and forgo uranium enrichment and reprocessing activities that can be used to develop nuclear weapons. By working with other nations under the Global Nuclear Energy Partnership, we can provide safe, cheap, and reliable energy that growing economies need—while reducing the risk of nuclear proliferation.

GNEP also will help resolve nuclear waste disposal issues. Based on technological advancements that would be made through GNEP, the volume and radio-toxicity of waste requiring permanent disposal at Yucca Mountain [Nevada] could be greatly reduced, eliminating the need for an additional repository. It is important to emphasize, however, that GNEP does not diminish in any way the need for, or the urgency of, the nuclear waste disposal program at Yucca Mountain. Yucca Mountain is still required under any fuel cycle scenario.

Renewable Solar and Wind Energy

Solar energy is clean, abundant, widespread, and renewable. Various technologies can capture this solar energy, concentrate it, store it, and convert it into other useful forms of energy. Concentrating Solar Power (CSP) devices optically focus or concentrate the thermal energy of the sun to drive a generator or heat an engine. They do so by means of lenses or mirrors arranged in a trough or tower configuration. Solar water heating systems directly absorb the sun's radiation with specially-coated absorbers to heat air or water for use in a building. Solar water heaters can be used in large commercial applications or in low-profile installations on residences anywhere in the United States.

Photovoltaic (PV) devices generate electricity directly from sunlight via an electronic process that occurs naturally in certain types of material. Electrons in certain types of crystals are freed by solar energy and can be induced to travel through an electrical circuit, powering any type of electronic device or load. PV devices can be used to power small devices (e.g., road signs and calculators), homes, or even large stores or businesses. Worldwide growth rates for PV . . . have averaged well over 35%, meaning the amount of installed power doubles every 4 years or less. However, this rapid growth is from a very small base; PV still accounts for less than 1 percent of electricity generation worldwide. Emerging technologies, such as "solar shingles" where PV cells are embedded into roofing materials, offer the prospect of "zero-net energy homes," which on average create as much energy as they consume.

To fulfill solar energy's promise, the President's 2007 Budget proposes a new $148 million Solar America Initiative—an increase of $65 million over FY06 [fiscal year 2006]. The Solar America Initiative will accelerate the development of advanced photovoltaic materials that convert sunlight directly to electricity, with the goal of making solar PV cost-competitive with other forms of renewable electricity by 2015. As the per-unit cost for these advanced PV technologies falls, sales volume will go up, driving new innovation and further cost reductions. Globally, attempts to bring electricity to the developing world will frequently employ solar PV as the lowest-cost alternative.

Wind energy is one of the world's fastest-growing energy technologies. In 2005, the U.S. wind energy industry installed more than 2,300 megawatts (MW) of new wind energy capacity—or over $3 billion worth of new generating equipment—in 22 states. Areas with good-wind resources have the potential to supply up to 20% of the electricity consumption of the United States.

In response to a recommendation in the President's 2001 National Energy Policy, the Bureau of Land Management (BLM) prepared a programmatic Environmental Impact Statement (EIS) to evaluate issues associated with wind energy development on Western public lands (excluding Alaska) administered by the BLM. The EIS, which was finalized in late 2005, implements a Wind Energy Development Program within the Department of the Interior, establishes policies and best management practices for wind energy right-of-way authorizations, and amends 52 BLM land-use plans in Colorado, Idaho, Montana, Nevada, New Mexico, Oregon, Utah, Washington, and Wyoming to set aside areas of significant wind energy potential for further development.

To expand the generation of clean energy from wind, the President's 2007 Budget includes $44 million for wind energy research, a $5 million increase over FY06 levels. This will help improve the efficiency and lower the costs of conventional wind turbine technologies; it will also help develop new small-scale wind technologies for use in low-speed wind environments. Combined with the ongoing efforts to expand access to Federal lands for wind energy development, this new funding will help dramatically increase the use of wind energy in the United States.

Periodical Bibliography

The following articles have been selected to supplement the diverse views presented in this chapter.

Alan Bailey	"North Slope Gas Hydrates Starting to Look Feasible," *Petroleum News*, January 2005. www.petroleumnews.com/.
Jesse Broehl	"Solar Granted a Major Victory in Energy Bill," Renewable Energy Access, July 29, 2005. www.renewableenergyaccess.com/.
Paul Brown	"Micro-Power Hailed as Cheap, Safe Energy of Future," *Guardian* (Manchester, UK), June 29, 2005. http://politics.guardian.co.uk/.
Jack Coleman	"The Sound and Visions of the Wind," *Cape Cod Today*, May 25, 2005.
Jeff Deyette	"Flip the Switch to Green Power," *Catalyst*, Fall 2003.
Paul Gipe	"Sobering Altamont Bird Report Issued," Wind-Works, March 14, 2004. www.wind-works.org/.
Peter Li	"Green School Is a Good Neighbor," *School Planning and Management*, May 2005.
Mother Earth News	"Plug in the Sun," August/September 2003. www.motherearthnews.com/
Popular Mechanics	"Fuel from Ice That Burns," December 2000.
Christine Real de Azua	"The Power of a Breeze: Wind Energy Is Coming of Age in the United States," *Buildings*, March 2005.
Jerry Reynolds	"Wind Power Gets Attention as Energy Picture Changes," *Indian Country Today*, February 25, 2005.
David Suzuki	"They're Welcome in My Backyard," *New Scientist*, April 16, 2005.

OPPOSING
VIEWPOINTS®
SERIES

CHAPTER 4

Should Alternatives to Fossil Fuels Be Pursued?

Chapter Preface

Domestic oil supplies have been diminishing since the 1960s, and as of 2000 the United States imports 56 percent of the petroleum it consumes. But despite growing awareness of the finite supply of oil in the world, the number of gas-powered vehicles—especially SUVs, trucks, and other large vehicles with low fuel efficiency—has been continually increasing in the United States. The huge numbers of vehicles on the road today emit immense quantities of CO_2 and other so-called greenhouse gases, increasing air pollution and, according to many scientists, contributing to possibly catastrophic global warming. This trend is not limited to the United States: As workers' incomes grow with industrialization, the number of gas-powered vehicles in China has likewise increased dramatically, causing historic traffic jams and unhealthy levels of air pollution.

Governments are hard pressed to develop policies that both conserve supplies of petroleum fuels and supply the thirsty world's gasoline-engine automobiles. In the Energy Policy Act of 2005, federal officials declined to set minimum automobile fuel-economy standards, instead offering tax incentives to the oil and gas industry for increasing gasoline-fuel efficiency. The act also encourages the development of alternative fuels known as biofuels—fuels derived from renewable biological materials such as plants and treated municipal waste. Biofuels include methanol and the best-known and potentially most promising fuel, ethanol.

In the United States, ethanol is made from cellulose feedstocks such as corn stalks, rice straw, sugar cane, bagasse, pulpwood, switchgrass, and municipal solid waste. Brazil, which has major pollution problems in its cities, is the world's lead producer of biofuels, deriving ethanol from sugar cane. Various blends of ethanol and gasoline make up biofuels and biodiesel, ranging from 5 percent to 15 percent ethanol. The act mandates that annual production of renewable fuels grow to 7.5 billion gallons by 2012, most of which is expected to come from ethanol. This figure pales beside total annual U.S. gasoline consumption figures of 140 billion gallons (in 2004), however, and alternative fuel producers are lobbying hard for additional supports.

Alternatives to gas-powered cars are available—electric-powered, natural-gas-powered, and even air-powered prototypes exist in limited supply—but detractors claim these alternatives are not efficient, economical, or clean. However, proponents maintain that driving alternative-fuel-powered vehicles is essential to reduce U.S. dependence on imported oil and improve air quality. According to the Union of Concerned Scientists, hybrid vehicles, designed to run on various combinations of gasoline and other energy sources—will fill in the gap and provide a stepping-stone to zero-emission vehicles. For example, hybrid trucks that raise fuel economy from 20 miles per gallon to 34 miles per gallon could save up to 9.3 million gallons of gasoline a year.

In recent years hydrogen has drawn the attention of scientists, politicians, and alternative-fuel enthusiasts as a new, clean energy source, but a "hydrogen economy" with zero-emission vehicles is not around the corner, according to science writer Michael Behar. Behar argues that no single fuel alternative will solve the energy crisis, and urges development of a portfolio of energy-efficient technologies to liberate the world from fossil fuels and ease global warming. In the following chapter, experts debate the merits and drawbacks of replacement fuels to meet the world's transportation needs.

| "*Progress in commercialising hydrogen technology is advancing rapidly.*"

Hydrogen Can Replace Petroleum-Based Automotive Fuels

Tom Nicholls

In the following viewpoint, Tom Nicholls argues that the commercial use of hydrogen as fuel—especially in cars—is imminent. Nicholls acknowledges that hydrogen fuel-cell technology is still in its infancy, but he notes that several automakers have announced that they expect hydrogen-fueled vehicles to become viable alternatives to gasoline-powered ones sometime between 2010 and 2020. Tom Nicholls is the editor of Petroleum Economist, *an international energy journal.*

As you read, consider the following questions:

1. Who dominates research and development in hydrogen fuel-cells, according to Nicholls?
2. What is the FreedomCAR Initiative, as explained by the author?
3. According to the author, which country aims to be the first to establish a hydrogen economy?

Progress in commercialising hydrogen technology is advancing rapidly. Stationary fuel cells could be supplying domestic energy needs as early as [2004], while hydrogen-powered cars could be on sale by the end of the decade.

Fuel Cells, in which hydrogen and oxygen combine in an electrochemical reaction to produce water, generating electricity, are surprisingly close to commercial application. Cars powered by hydrogen could be available as soon as 2010 and in widespread use by 2020. Stationary fuel cells, for supplying energy to businesses and homes, are much closer to becoming a profitable business proposition—manufacturers hope to start selling products around the middle of the decade.

Momentum in the research and development (R&D) process—dominated by Japan, Europe and North America—suggests the economics of fuel cells are promising. Energy companies are forming business units dedicated to hydrogen and putting financial muscle into R&D. Rivalry among the world's main car companies to produce the first affordable and reliable fuel cell car is intense. Governments are supplying more and more funding.

Government Support

The US government gave fuel cells . . . a significant boost in January [2003], when hydrogen technology formed an important part of President George [W.] Bush's State of the Union speech. Bush said the government would provide $1.7bn [billion] (including $0.72bn in new spending) for R&D funding for vehicles and stationary units over the [period 2003–2008].

The rewards for all could be considerable in terms of efficiency, the environment and energy supply security.

According to UTC Fuel Cells (UTCFC), one of the world's main fuel cell manufacturers, electrical efficiency is 40%, rising to 80% if the heat is also recovered. Fuel efficiency in fuel cell cars is also much higher than in conventional vehicles. In terms of operation (tank-to-wheel efficiency), a fuel cell is about twice as efficient as a gasoline-fired internal-combustion engine. In addition, it is generally thought that overall efficiency, taking into account the source of the hydrogen (well-to-wheel efficiency), can also be higher. . . .

Public-Private Partnership

The extra US government spending—allocated under the FreedomCAR (Cooperative Automotive Research) and Fuel Initiative (FFI)—builds on FreedomCAR, a partnership between the government and the private sector founded in early 2002 with the aim of making fuel cell cars commonplace in the US by 2020 and cost-competitive with gasoline vehicles by 2010. The DOE [Department of Energy] estimates FFI could reduce GHG [greenhouse gases] emissions from transportation in the US by over 0.5bn tonnes of carbon equivalent a year by 2040, with additional reductions resulting from the use of fuel cells in other applications. It could also represent important energy supply security for the US by reducing its dependence—a national priority—on foreign sources of oil. The DOE believes oil imports could be cut by over 11m [million] b/d [barrels per day] by 2040 (at present, imports amount to 10m–11m b/d).

In order to attain the various desirable end-results, there is a lot of work still to do. For a start, hydrogen, when produced from natural gas, is four times as expensive to produce as gasoline, according to the DOE.

Making Fuel Cells Affordable

Government subsidies will reinforce the technology's economics, but affordability remains the biggest stumbling block, along with durability and reliability. Stationary units are the closest to market entry. There are several types of fuel cell with a variety of possible applications, but attention is focused on the Proton Exchange Membrane (PEM) system (also called Polymer Electrolyte Fuel Cell system—PEFC). Compared with other types of fuel cell, PEM units are smaller, easier to manufacture, operate at much lower temperatures and have greater commercial possibilities, such as supplying homes. They are being developed for cars, so scientific breakthroughs in the automotive field can be transferred to stationary applications, streamlining research and reducing costs. In the production phase, cost savings through mass production in the auto industry can also be transferred to the stationary sector.

Reliable and Affordable

"We will be able to make a practical, reliable and affordable fuel cell by 2005," says Toshiya Ohmura, manager of the Japan Gas Association's (JGA) fuel cell and hydrogen project department. JGA is taking an active role in R&D and aims to promote the use of fuel cells powered by hydrogen produced from natural gas. . . .

The problems for fuel cell car manufacturers are even greater [than affordability]. Part of the difficulty of successfully marketing fuel cell cars is that conventional gasoline and diesel cars have become so sophisticated in performance and cost. They will inevitably be the benchmark for hydrogen cars and, if they do not match up, consumers will not buy them.

In technical terms, operating conditions are much more onerous and space is restricted. "The environment under which a fuel cell must perform in a car is much more harrowing than a stationary application, which does not move and starts and stops once every few months," says [Jim] Bolch [vice president of UTCFC]. "In a car, it needs to be able to provide acceleration, deal with cold weather, hot weather, vibration and people driving their cars up onto the pavement. It is a much more challenging environment."

Commercial Viability by 2010

Although significant savings will come from mass production, cost-reductions are essential—Honda says the cost of producing a fuel cell car is 100 times the cost of producing a conventional vehicle. "We expect fuel cell cars to be commercial in 10–20 years from now," a company spokesman says, but adds that there "must be a technical breakthrough" before they can enter widespread use. Similarly, DaimlerChrysler expects "a broad market entry" of fuel cell vehicles after 2010.

The Japanese government also expects rapid expansion in the fuel cell car marketplace in the next decade. Its target for fuel cell cars in the domestic market is 50,000 by 2010 out of a total population of 70m cars and for 5m vehicles by 2020.

Car companies are taking a range of different approaches to fuel cells. In Honda's vehicles, a fuel cell powers the car using hydrogen stored in a tank. Toyota is developing hybrid vehicles that have an electric motor powered by a fuel cell and by a secondary battery, a system it claims has a superior well-to-wheel efficiency to that of vehicles powered only by fuel cells. Germany's BMW, meanwhile, has adopted a very different approach and is trying to develop an internal-combustion engine that burns hydrogen instead of fossil fuels. A separate fuel cell in the same vehicle would power the car's electrical devices. Given the lack of hydrogen refuelling facilities, the firm is developing so-called dual-fuel cars. These are able to run off gasoline or hydrogen and are fitted with separate tanks for each fuel.

The Need for Refuelling Networks

Regardless of the system individual companies adopt, hydrogen vehicles also need refuelling networks, which will be expensive to build. Alternatives are: refuelling stations that use methane (or other hydrocarbons) as a feedstock, which is reformed on site, allowing vehicles to be filled directly with hydrogen; [steam] reforming systems sited on-board vehicles that fill up with hydrocarbons; or, if fuel cells are widely distributed among households, cars could be charged at home. Initially, cars will refuel with hydrogen. This will require improvements in compression technology so that cars can drive a reasonable distance without having to refuel (as a light gas, hydrogen's energy density is much lower than that of liquid fuels).

On-board reforming is an attractive option for the longer term as it limits the need for new hydrogen infrastructure and on-board hydrogen compression, but it would be technically very difficult because of the operating conditions. "With on-board reforming, you are asking a vehicle to behave like a refinery and it is a challenging chemical-engineering issue to get everything to work in a small space, the way you want it to work. Reforming itself is not difficult, but doing it in real-time and enabling the car to respond to the needs of a driver are considerable challenges," says David Jollie, editor, *Fuel Cell Today*.

According to Jollie, all the refuelling systems are possible and will depend on market circumstances, which may vary from region to region. "The various systems all have separate benefits and it is not impossible for all of them to be used. It will be a question of what the market pull is and what the interests of energy companies, customers and car companies are."

The infrastructure problem gives buses an advantage over cars, because they usually need only one, centralised fuelling point. As a result, they are likely to be commercialised first. UTCFC, for example, expects fleet vehicles to become an emerging market "in the 2005–2007 time-frame".

Fuel-cell bus programmes are driving the hydrogen R&D effort in Europe. The European Union's (EU) 18.5m euro ($19.9m) Clean Urban Transport for Europe demonstration project aims to help nine European cities introduce hydrogen into their public transportation system. The EU says the project, the largest fuel-cell bus demonstration project in the world, will address the issues of hydrogen production, refuelling in city centres and operational use in commercial public-transport systems. Buses will operate like normal buses, on the same lines and under the same tight time schedule to provide the best comparisons of performance and cost.

As part of Iceland's plan to become the world's first hydrogen economy, the Ectos project, which is being run by Icelandic New Energy (a business partnership involving Daimler-Chrysler, Norsk Hydro and Royal Dutch/Shell), is introducing three fuel cell buses to the public transport network. If tests are successful, Ectos' aim is to replace "a larger number" of Reykjavik city buses with hydrogen vehicles. . . .

Many other fuel cell popularisation programmes exist. Among the most important in North America is California Fuel Cell Partnership (CaFCP). The venture involves car, energy and fuel cell companies, and government agencies. CaFCP aims to have up to 60 fuel cell vehicles on the road by the end of 2003 (which will include some buses).[1] Its main aims are to: demonstrate the vehicle technology by operating and test ing under real-world conditions in California; demonstrate the viability of alternative fuel infrastructure technology, including hydrogen and methanol stations; explore the path to commercialisation, from identifying potential problems to developing solutions; and increase public awareness and enhance opinion about fuel cell electric vehicles, preparing the market for commercialisation.

---

1. The CaFCP has tested fifty-five cars in California and in 2005 experimented with a few buses on selected routes.

> "As a low-heating-value, low-boiling-point gas, [hydrogen] is inherently expensive to transport, store, and distribute—all strong disadvantages for a transportation fuel."

Hydrogen Is Impractical as an Automotive Fuel

David W. Keith and Alexander E. Farrell

In the following viewpoint, David W. Keith and Alexander E. Farrell argue against the rush to embrace hydrogen as the automotive fuel of the future. They point out several significant disadvantages of hydrogen as automobile fuel: It is expensive, cannot be easily stored, and would be much more cost-effective for heavy freight vehicles than for cars. The authors suggest that strategic petroleum reserves and petroleum substitutes are better options than hydrogen to ensure American energy security. David W. Keith holds the Canada Research Chair in the Department of Chemical and Petroleum Engineering at the University of Calgary. Alexander E. Farrell is an assistant professor in the Energy and Resources Group of the University of California at Berkeley. Both men are also adjunct faculty members of the Department of Engineering and Public Policy at Carnegie Mellon University in Pittsburgh.

David W. Keith and Alexander E. Farrell, "Rethinking Hydrogen Cars," *Science*, vol. 301, July 18, 2003, pp. 315–16. Copyright 2003 by AAAS. Reproduced by permission.

As you read, consider the following questions:

1. According to the authors, what makes hydrogen so costly to store and transport?
2. According to Keith and Farrell, why are strategic petroleum reserves a better option than hydrogen cars for securing energy resources?
3. Which petroleum substitutes do the authors favor instead of hydrogen for cars?

Support for hydrogen cars has reached new heights, especially for fuel-cell vehicles that use hydrogen directly. The largest effort is President [George W.] Bush's FreedomCAR and Fuel Initiative, which amounts to $1.7 billion over 5 years. Critics suggest the plan is a tactical move to avoid policies such as strict fuel efficiency standards that could be readily implemented today. Here, we take a longer-term strategic view of energy policy and argue against early adoption of hydrogen cars.

The introduction of any new transportation fuel is a rare, difficult, and uncertain venture—it demands a linked introduction of a new fuel distribution system and new vehicles, because neither is useful without the other. Although technically feasible, a hydrogen refueling infrastructure would be expensive: initial cost would likely exceed $5000 per vehicle even if one assumes large economies of scale. The cars themselves will also likely be expensive. If hydrogen cars are ever to match the performance of current vehicles at a reasonable cost— particularly fueling convenience, range, and size—technological breakthroughs in hydrogen storage and energy conversion will be required.

Like electricity, hydrogen is an energy carrier that must be produced from a primary energy source. Today, hydrogen is produced from natural gas on a large scale and at low cost: hydrogen production consumes $\sim$2% of U.S. primary energy, and at the point of production, it costs less than gasoline per-unit of energy. Although hydrogen production is simple, as a low-heating-value, low-boiling-point gas, it is inherently expensive to transport, store, and distribute—all strong disadvantages for a transportation fuel.

Hydrogen offers three principal advantages that may offset its disadvantages and may address important policy goals: (i) it can be burned cleanly or used in fuel cells and so can reduce air pollution; (ii) it emits no CO_2 [carbon dioxide] at point of use; and (iii) it can be produced from diverse energy sources and so can reduce oil dependence.

Air Quality

Hydrogen could essentially eliminate vehicular emissions, but the cost of reducing NO_x [nitrogen oxides] emissions (for example) with hydrogen will be on the order of $1 million per tonne of NO_2 [nitric oxide]. In contrast, meeting the EPA's [Environmental Protection Agency] new Tier 2 standards will reduce emissions for about $2000 per tonne, and inspection and maintenance programs will cost about $4000 per tonne and scrappage programs (voluntary programs offering bounties for old vehicles), less than $10,000 per tonne. The cost of reducing NO_x emissions from electricity production is in the same range. Similar comparisons can be made for other important air pollutants.

It is comparatively expensive to reduce pollutant emissions by using hydrogen because regulation-driven technological innovation has reduced emissions from gasoline-powered cars to the point where they have very low emissions per-unit-energy compared with other sectors and other transportation modes. This trend will continue, reducing the benefit of zero-emission hydrogen vehicles, particularly because many technologies (e.g., electric drive) can be used on both platforms.

Hydrogen could largely eliminate the problem of "high emitters"—the few poorly designed or maintained cars that account for most automobile emission—because hydrogen cars do not have high-emission failure modes. Nevertheless, the approaches listed above, possibly in conjunction with roadside emission monitoring and other advanced techniques, provide far more cost-effective solutions.

Climate Change

A near-zero-emission source of hydrogen is required if hydrogen cars are to reduce CO_2 emissions substantially. The cost of CO_2-neutral hydrogen turns on the viability of CO_2 capture and storage (CCS) because it is currently much cheaper to make hydrogen from fossil feedstocks such as coal or gas than from other sources. It is substantially easier to capture CO_2 from hydrogen production than from electric power plants because the CO_2 is at high partial pressure—indeed many existing facilities already vent nearly pure CO_2. If CO_2 storage in geological reservoirs (or perhaps elsewhere) is socially acceptable and can be widely implemented, then the cost premium for CO_2-neutral hydrogen will likely be less than 30%. Even with these assumptions, hydrogen cars will be an expensive CO_2 mitigation option because of the high cost of vehicles and refueling infrastructure. Costs may exceed $1000 per tonne of carbon if hydrogen cars are to match the performance of evolved conventional vehicles. With consistent assumptions about CCS, reducing electric sector emissions by 50%— equivalent to eliminating CO_2 emissions from all cars—is likely to cost between $75 and $150/tC [per tonne of carbon].

If CCS proves unacceptable, the cost of reducing CO_2 emissions with hydrogen cars will be much higher. Electrolysis using non-fossil electricity is a leading option, but it places substantial extra costs and inefficiencies between energy source and end use. Until CO_2 emissions from electricity generation are virtually eliminated, it will be far more cost-effective to use new CO_2-neutral electricity (e.g., wind or nuclear) to reduce emissions by substituting for fossil-generated electricity.

Cartoon by Mike Keefe. Reproduced by Cagle Cartoons.

Therefore, whether CCS is viable or not, it will be more cost-effective to reduce CO_2 emissions in the electric sector than to do so using hydrogen cars. For several decades, the most cost-effective method to reduce CO_2 emissions from cars will be to increase fuel efficiency. A recent National Academy of Sciences study concluded, for example, that 12 to 42% improvements in the fuel economy of light-duty vehicles would pay for themselves in lifetime fuel savings, and these estimates probably understate the potential because they exclude diesels and hybrids.

Energy Security

Improving fuel efficiency would help moderate oil consumption along with CO_2 emissions. In addition, there are two other options to increase energy security: strategic petroleum reserves (SPRs) and petroleum substitutes. Several industrial countries have SPRs to manage supply interruptions; the U.S. alone stores about 50 days worth of imports. However, management of SPR assets has been relatively ineffective. Proposals to use the SPR to limit price spikes, rather than ill-defined "emergencies," to allow market participants to bid on new SPR options contracts, or to turn SPR management over to an independent agency all deserve serious consideration.

Petroleum substitutes include synthetic hydrocarbon fuels [synfuels] derived from fossil feed-stocks (coal) or from biomass including cellulosic bio-ethanol and bio-diesel. It has long been assumed that manufacture of synfuels from coal would produce unacceptably large CO_2 emissions, but as with hydrogen production, CCS could change the game because it is comparatively easy to capture CO_2 from synfuel production. Indeed, CO_2 from the major U.S. coal-to-gas facility is currently being captured and stored. Bio-fuel production with CCS would have net negative CO_2 emissions, which could lower the cost of mitigation.

Such petroleum substitutes are cost-competitive with hydrogen, and because they can be stored, transported, and distributed through the existing infrastructure and used in existing vehicles, they can be introduced more quickly with much less technological risk than could hydrogen.

Hydrogen's Role as a Transportation Fuel

Global CO_2 emissions must decline by about an order of magnitude [by ten times] in order to stabilize atmospheric concentrations, so major emission reductions will eventually be required from cars. Cost-effective climate policy, however, starts with low-cost emissions reductions and proceeds at a measured pace. Analysis of optimal climate policy typically shows that to stabilize concentrations below a doubling of preindustrial levels, overall emissions do not need to be reduced by more than 30% below business-as-usual until after 2040. When emission mitigation opportunities across the economy are ordered by their cost (to form a supply curve), deep reductions in automobile emissions are not in the cheapest 30%. All else [being] equal, it is therefore wasteful to devote substantial resources to achieving deep reductions in auto emissions until after 2040. Only then will radical new technologies likely be needed. Hydrogen cars should be seen as one of several long-run options, but they make no sense any time soon.

If we were certain that hydrogen fuel was the only long-run solution to eliminating CO_2 emissions from cars, then it might make sense to focus R&D [research and development] now, even though widespread deployment is decades away. If, however, we accept that there is considerable uncertainty about the optimum long-run solution, then early commitment to hydrogen fuel is unwise because it risks technological lock-in.

If it were necessary to introduce hydrogen into the transportation sector, a wiser strategy would focus on transportation modes other than cars. Hydrogen-powered heavy freight vehicles, such as ships, trains, and large trucks, could provide greater air-quality benefits (they have much higher emission intensities) and could be more easily implemented (they require a much smaller distribution infrastructure) and make less stringent demands on the performance of hydrogen storage systems (onboard space has a smaller premium).

Despite the arguments presented above and despite criticism of tactical aspects of the Administration's new programs, there is a deep and widespread interest in hydrogen cars. An unusual coalition—from environmentalists and futurists to auto executives, oil barons, and nuclear engineers—advocates the deployment of hydrogen cars as a long-run strategic goal for climate and energy policy, and many share a broader vision of a "hydrogen economy." However, enthusiasm for hydrogen cars conceals widely divergent visions of the future aimed at incompatible goals. Some would like to manufacture hydrogen using nuclear power, others using solar energy. Some seek energy independence, others, to stop climate change.

The appeal of hydrogen arises, in part, because it is a pristine high-technology solution that promises to resolve multiple problems simultaneously by making a clean break from present technologies and avoiding long-standing controversies over issues like drilling in the Arctic National Wildlife Reserve and emissions from sport utility vehicles (SUVs). It is an attractive vision that demands serious investigation, but it's not a sure thing. Transportation R&D should be broadly based, and should focus on basic enabling technologies rather than on a rush to deploy hydrogen cars.

Finally, research must not stand in the way of action. Near-term strategies to address the serious challenges posed by air pollution, climate change, and petroleum dependence should focus on emissions from electricity generation and freight transport, on strategic petroleum reserves, on energy efficiency, and on petroleum substitutes.

| "*Alternative fuels are the most promising technologies in the long run, since they could virtually eliminate oil use in cars and trucks.*"

Alternatives to Fossil Fuels Are the Long-Term Energy Solution

David Friedman

David Friedman is a senior analyst in the Union of Concerned Scientists' Clean Vehicles Program. In the following viewpoint, Friedman argues that America's unabated appetite for oil and its dependence on foreign oil imports, as well as the serious and challenging environmental problems that are the consequences of fossil-fuel use, require immediate and fundamental changes in transportation, the greatest single user of fossil fuels. Friedman calls for significant investment in hybrid vehicles, hydrogen fuel cells, and alternative fuels. Hybrid vehicles, he maintains, while not a perfect solution, will bridge the gap and buy time to develop zero-emission vehicles before the oil runs out.

David Friedman, *A New Road: The Technology and Potential of Hybrid Vehicles*. Cambridge, MA: Union of Concerned Scientists, 2003. Reproduced by permission.

As you read, consider the following questions:

1. How much of the oil imported into the United States is consumed by car and truck fuel, according to Friedman?

2. According to the author, how can hybrid vehicles play a key role in curbing oil demand and global-warming emissions?

3. Why was the public not ready to accept hybrid vehicles when they were introduced in 1997, but is ready to accept them now, according to Friedman?

The world started down a new road in 1997 when the first modern hybrid electric car, the Toyota Prius, was sold in Japan. Two years later, the United States saw its first sale of a hybrid, the Honda Insight. These two vehicles, followed by the Honda Civic Hybrid, marked a radical change in the type of car being offered to the public: vehicles that bring some of the benefits of battery electric vehicles into the conventional gasoline-powered cars and trucks we have been using for more than 100 years.

While hybrids are not as clean and efficient as vehicles powered by hydrogen fuel cells or solely by batteries, they offer both lower emissions than today's conventional vehicles and dramatically higher fuel economy. And they provide a stepping-stone to zero emission vehicles.

Today, four years after their introduction, many of us know something about hybrids, but many of our questions remain unanswered: What exactly is a hybrid vehicle? How good will hybrids' fuel economy and environmental performance be? How fast will they go? What will they cost? Will people buy them? And where do you plug them in? The answer to the last question is simple: you don't have to! (For some this will be a disappointment, for others, a relief.) The answers to the other questions are more complicated. This [viewpoint] provides some of those answers.

Why Hybrids?

The primary importance of hybrid technology for cars and trucks is its potential to increase fuel economy dramatically while meeting today's most stringent tailpipe emission standards (excluding the zero emission vehicle standard). At the same time, the performance of hybrid vehicles can equal or even surpass that of most conventional vehicles. Moreover, hybrids can play a critical role in helping bring the technology of motors, power electronics, and batteries to maturity and in reducing their cost. Such changes are vital to the success of future hydrogen fuel cell and other zero emission vehicles.

Thus hybrids could be a key element in US strategies to address our growing energy insecurity and environmental problems. Whether hybrids live up to their potential hinges on automakers and governments embracing them as one means of moving toward a secure energy future and a healthier environment.

The size of our oil dependence and its rate of growth, as well as the environmental problems that are its consequence, require an immediate response. This calls for both changes in conventional technology and a longer-term investment in hybrid vehicles, hydrogen fuel cells, and alternative fuels.

In the year 2000, the United States consumed nearly 20 million barrels of oil products every day.[. . .] Over half of that was supplied by other countries, including Iraq, Saudi Arabia, and other nations in the politically unstable Middle East. Of that daily consumption, 40% (about 8 million barrels per day) went to fuel our cars and trucks, at a cost to consumers of $186 billion. By 2020, oil consumption is expected to grow by nearly 40% and our dependence on imports is projected to rise to more than 60%.

Those same cars and trucks were responsible for over 20% of the global warming emissions produced by the United States during 2000: 1,450 million tons (358 million metric tons, carbon equivalent) of the heat-trapping gases linked to

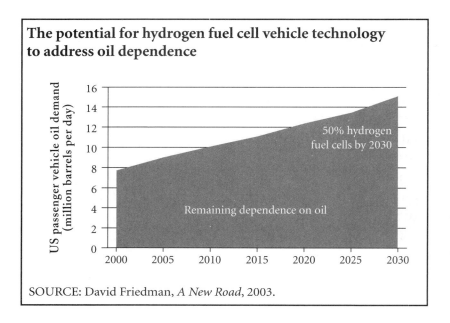

The potential for hydrogen fuel cell vehicle technology to address oil dependence

US passenger vehicle oil demand (million barrels per day)

50% hydrogen fuel cells by 2030

Remaining dependence on oil

SOURCE: David Friedman, *A New Road*, 2003.

global warming. Most of these gases will stay in the atmosphere for more than 170 years, contributing to an increase in the earth's average surface temperature. This is projected to rise 2.5 to 10.4°F (1.4 to 5.8°C) between 1990 and 2100, if no major efforts are undertaken to reduce emissions of global warming gases. As the earth continues to warm, we face a great risk that the climate will change in ways that threaten our health, our economy, our farms and forests, beaches and wetlands, and other natural habitats.

Air Pollution

Cars and trucks are also major contributors to air pollution. Regulations have helped clean up passenger vehicles over the past three decades. However, rising demand for travel and increased vehicle ownership will outpace even the standards on the books through this decade. Cars and trucks will need to clean up their act even more if we are to eliminate the threat air pollution poses to public health—especially to our children and the elderly.

Finally, producing and distributing the gasoline that went to fuel our cars and trucks in the year 2000 resulted in the emission of 848,000 tons of smog-forming pollutants and 392,000 tons of benzene-equivalent toxic chemicals, in addition to the pollutants emitted from the tailpipes of vehicles. Altogether, cars and trucks are the largest single source of air pollution in most urban areas. As with U.S. oil use and global warming emissions, upstream air pollution is expected to continue to rise significantly over the next two decades, posing the greatest health threat to children, the elderly, and other vulnerable members of our population.

The situation is urgent, but not hopeless. A range of technological approaches can help us break free of our oil habit and protect our health and livelihood against the environmental problems associated with vehicle use. Hybrid technology is one of the most promising.

No single silver bullet can solve the problems posed by our use of cars and trucks. But if we choose now to invest in a variety of solutions, ranging from near to long term, together they could eliminate the use of oil for transportation. Hybrid technology can fill the midterm gap between immediate improvements to conventional vehicle fuel economy and the long-term hope offered by hydrogen fuel cells and alternative fuels.

The quickest and most effective way to limit oil dependence during the next 10 to 15 years is to improve the fuel economy of gasoline-fueled cars and trucks. Analysis of existing and emerging technologies based on reports by the National Academy of Sciences, researchers at MIT [the Massachusetts Institute of Technology], and others indicates that conventional fuel economy technology can enable conventional cars and trucks to reach an average of 40 miles per gallon before the middle of the next decade. Moreover, this can be done cost effectively.

With more efficient engines, improved transmissions, and better aerodynamics and tires, automakers could reach a fleet average of 40 mpg [miles per gallon] over the next ten years. At that rate of implementation, passenger vehicle oil use would stop growing by 2007, stabilizing at today's level through 2020. This would save consumers billions of dollars every year, effectively paying us to reduce our oil habit and our impact on the environment.

Conventional fuel economy technologies are thus a good short-term investment in energy security and the environment. But if we stopped there, after 2020 increases in the number of miles traveled and the number of vehicles on the road would begin to overwhelm the fuel economy improvements and oil use would again rise. Thus a long-term investment strategy is necessary.

Hydrogen Fuel Cells

Hydrogen fuel cells and alternative fuels are the most promising technologies in the long run, since they could virtually eliminate oil use in cars and trucks. But they are not yet available and are unlikely to reach significant market penetration for 10 to 15 years. Moreover, while these technologies will shift us off oil, they will not make as rapid progress toward eliminating cars' and trucks' global warming emissions. For example, during the first decades after fuel cells are introduced, the hydrogen they use is likely to be produced from natural gas. This will result in lower, but still substantial emissions of global warming gases.

Today's vehicles stay on the roads an average of 15 years, so waiting 10 to 15 years for hydrogen fuel cell or other alternative fuel technologies would mean locking ourselves into a path of increased oil dependence and environmental problems for the next 20 to 30 years.

Since hydrogen fuel cells are not yet right around the corner, the best solution in the very near term is to bring more advanced conventional technologies to the marketplace. At the same time, we will need to prepare for the long term by investing in developing and demonstrating hydrogen fuel cells and alternative fuels.

But that's not enough. This scenario leaves a gap of ten or more years without significant progress in reducing our oil dependence. While that's not a good prospect, the consequence for climate change is worse, since the severity of global warming is a function of cumulative global warming gases. Every ton of global warming gas that could have been avoided is another ton that will remain in the atmosphere for the next 100 years. Since hydrogen fuel cell vehicles are likely to deliver only modest global warming emission savings by 2030, another technology is needed as the gains from conventional technology level off in the next decade.

With their recent entrance into the market, hybrids are poised to serve a key role in pushing down oil demand and global warming emissions from cars and trucks through the next two decades. They offer a solid midterm strategy of investment in energy security and the environment, filling the temporal gap between conventional technology and hydrogen fuel cells.

Hybrids can also serve as an insurance policy for regulators contemplating significant increases to fuel economy standards over the next decade. While a 40-mpg fleet could be reached with existing conventional technology, hybrid vehicles provide additional assurance of reaching that goal, since they promise fuel economy levels as high as 50 to 60 mpg. Further, they open the door to fuel economy standards of 50 mpg or higher by the end of the next decade.

In addition, hybrid vehicles can mitigate the risk of delays in hydrogen fuel cell development and market success. They'll also help ensure the success of fuel cell vehicles by bringing down the costs of the technologies—motors, batteries, and power electronics—that the two share. And they'll help pave the way by acquainting consumers with electric drive technology.

Given the necessity of continuing to reduce oil use and global warming emissions over the coming decades, hybrids are a key interim step, taking over where improved conventional technologies leave off and before fuel cells can fulfill their promise.

The "Gee-Whiz" Factor

In addition to the logic of hybrids as a key part of investing in energy security and the environment, other factors, such as consumer and automaker choice, could prove crucial to their success.

Despite automakers' claims to the contrary, consumers are showing interest in having an option to buy cars and trucks with better fuel economy. A consumer preference study by J.D. Power and Associates found that 30% of the more than 5,000 recent new-vehicle buyers they surveyed would definitely consider a hybrid for their next purchase. An additional 30% showed strong consideration. The primary reason people noted for considering a hybrid was their concern about high fuel prices.

A second study, by Applied Decision Analysis LLC, performed as part of a larger study on hybrids by the Electric Power Research Institute, found that 25% of the 400 potential car and truck buyers surveyed would purchase a hybrid vehicle instead of a conventional vehicle when given information on the potential costs, savings, and performance of the hybrid.

Clearly, consumers want automakers to provide them with hybrid vehicles as additional choices when they step into the showroom.

Automaker Choice

Only Toyota and Honda have so far offered hybrids for sale in the US market. Both are likely to offer more models very soon, as are most other automakers. . . .

These new vehicles will help build the hybrid market, bringing in consumers interested in pickups or SUVs as well as those who want compact and family cars. But if some of the automakers choose to offer vehicles with hybrid name-plates just to capitalize on the "gee whiz" factor or the "green" image of hybrids, much of the potential benefits from hybrid technology will be lost. Automakers have a responsibility to society and consumers to market hybrids that provide the dramatic improvements in fuel economy the technology promises, along with substantially cleaner tailpipe emissions. And consumers must hold them to it, by putting their dollars where they will do the most good.

The next decade may see a revolution in which the automobile industry offers consumers more choices than ever before. But predicting the exact role hybrid vehicles will play in transportation's future is beyond the scope of this [viewpoint].

"The day of the biofuel has arrived. . . .
For the user, biofuels are currently
cheaper [than fossil fuels]."

Biofuels Are Clean and Affordable Alternatives

Vivaj V. Vaitheeswaran

Vivaj V. Vaitheeswaran is the global environment and energy
consultant for the British magazine Economist *and the author*
of Power to the People: How the Coming Energy Revolution
Will Transform an Industry, Change Our Lives, and Maybe
Even Save the Planet. *In the following viewpoint, Vaitheeswaran*
shows that as fossil fuels become more expensive and more scarce,
biofuels—fuels derived from plants—become significantly more
attractive. The author traces the history of two biofuels that are
attracting particular attention, biodiesel and ethanol.

As you read, consider the following questions:

1. According to Vaitheeswaran, why are biofuels considered renewable resources when fossil fuels are not?
2. Why is Brazil the world leader in production of biofuels, according to the author?

Vivaj V. Vaitheeswaran, "Stirrings in the Corn Fields: Biofuels," *Economist*, vol. 375, May 14, 2005, p. 71. Copyright © 2005 The Economist Newspaper Ltd. All rights reserved. Futher production prohibited. www. economist.com.

3. According to the author, why are carmakers willingly adapting their vehicles to these alternative fuels?

Pick your mix:

Diesel fuel made from oilseeds, petrol replaced by ethanol made from corn, sugar or grain—or even straw. They're here and are starting to change energy markets.

American output of maize-based ethanol is rising by 30% a year. Brazil, long the world leader, is pushing ahead as fast as the sugar crop from which its ethanol is made will allow. China, though late to start, has already built the world's biggest ethanol plant, and plans another as big. Germany, the big producer of biodiesel, is raising output 40–50% a year. France aims to triple output of the two fuels together by 2007. Even in backward Britain a smallish biodiesel plant has just come on stream, and another as big as Europe's biggest is being built. And after long research a Canadian firm has plans for a full-scale ethanol plant that will replace today's grain or sugar feedstock with straw. Output is still tiny compared with that of mineral fuels. But the day of the biofuel has arrived.

Currently Cheaper

The reason is simple. Forget greenery or energy security, the grounds on which governments justify subsidising biofuels. Just take [2004's] soaring price of mineral fuels, subtract the biofuel subsidy, and the answer is plain: for the user, biofuels are currently cheaper. Indeed, in America's corn (maize) states, locally produced ethanol is close to being competitive even without subsidy; imported Brazilian ethanol could have been so long ago, had not a federal tax credit for ethanol, originally 54 cents per American gallon, been carefully balanced by a 54 cent tariff.

Though production methods are rapidly evolving, the new fuels are new only in their rampant growth. An engine that

Rudolf Diesel showed at the 1900 World Exhibition in Paris ran on peanut oil, and biodiesel has been in small-scale use here and there since the 1930s. You can make it from animal fats, oilseeds, used cooking oil, sugar, grain and more. Indeed, you can feed your diesel vehicle with cooking oil from the supermarket and it will run, until (as they will) the filters gunge up. As for ethanol, Henry Ford was an enthusiast for crop-based ethanol in the 1920s.

Modern uses were sparked by the oil shock of 1973. Brazil, rich in sugar-cane but not oil, led the way, building cars adapted to burn pure ethanol until the late 1980s, when sliding oil prices and rising sugar prices made sugar a more profitable end-use for the cane growers and the subsidy for ethanol too costly for the state. In 1989–90 ethanol pumps began to run dry, and sales of these cars collapsed.

Today, both biofuels tend to be used in mixtures. Europeans typically use "B5"—standard diesel, blended with 5% biodiesel, usually made from rape[seed] (canola) oil. In America, many drivers, often unaware of it, are using E10 "gasohol"—10% ethanol, 90% standard gasoline.

But the proportions can be higher than that. Some American and Canadian public-sector vehicles run on B20. Californians use unmixed, 100% biodiesel, and, with additives to keep it usable down to −20°C, it is sold even in such colder places as Germany and Austria. As for ethanol, in its pure form it can damage standard gaskets and hoses. But, to meet Brazil's supply problems, carmakers there, already familiar with the stuff, in 2003 brought in "flex-fuel" engines that can run on any ethanol-petrol blend you like; at present 75% to 25% is standard. These now win 30% of new car sales there. The American version of flex-fuel runs on E85 (in practice, 70–85% ethanol, depending on the region and the season). Already America has 4m [million] such cars, and they are multiplying. So are E85 pumps for them. Indeed, the corn-state press delights in anecdotes of John Doe who habitually fills his ancient Chevy with E85 and avers that it suffers no harm.

If he's right, he is no fool: E85 (though not E10) gives a bit less oomph per gallon than standard fuel, but even so he is saving money. Supply constraints may prevent E85 being the future of ethanol in America. But if the oil price stays high, Mr Doe and other penny-pinchers will certainly be using more biofuel.

Pro-ethanol Pressure

The oil companies were originally far from happy to see "their" filling stations openly selling a rival fuel. They are still not eager. But pro-ethanol pressure has grown. America's environmentalists favour it (except the purists who object, truly enough, that the real "green" issue there is not the fuel but the cars that guzzle it). And the law, in some areas, is with them. Anti-smog rules require a clean-burn additive to petrol, and one formerly favoured, known as MTBE, turned out to have nasty properties, and is being phased out. Ethanol—as such, or used roughly half and half with another chemical in a compound known as ETBE—can do the job.

There is pressure too from the corn-growers, gleefully envisaging a huge new market; and hence from their politicians. The market is big already: of America's 255m tonnes of maize [in 2004], 30m went into ethanol. One or two states have adopted mandatory requirements for a certain use of this fuel; Minnesota requires E10 as a minimum, and its legislature has just voted to make that E20. A federal bill launched in [2005] calls for the use of 8 billion gallons of biofuels a year by 2012.

This and less ambitious bills are still merely bills, not law; and even 8 billion gallons, though near double [2005's] likely American output, looks trivial beside total motor fuel use, which already exceeds 175 billion gallons. Yet if oil stays high that target may be exceeded, law or no law, greens or no greens, because drivers will demand ethanol.

Ethanol Is the Answer

Instead of coming exclusively from corn or sugar cane as it has up to now, thanks to biotech breakthroughs, [ethanol] can be made out of everything from prairie switchgrass and wood chips to corn husks and other agricultural waste. This biomass-derived fuel is known as cellulosic ethanol. Whatever the source, burning ethanol instead of gasoline reduces carbon emissions by more than 80% while eliminating entirely the release of acid-rain-causing sulfur dioxide. Even the cautious Department of Energy predicts that ethanol could put a 30% dent in America's gasoline consumption by 2030.

Adam Lashinsky and Nathan D. Schwartz,
Fortune, January 24, 2006.

Do the Sums

The arithmetic is simple. Ethanol's federal tax credit is by now 51 cents per gallon. . . . So-called "small" producers, making up to 30m gallons a year, get an extra 10 cents. Several states add their own tax breaks, which can be worth 10–20 cents a gallon. Say, very crudely, 70 cents in all: 7 cents per gallon of E10, and nearly 60 cents for E85.

The subsidies in theory go mostly to the blender; how much in fact ends up with whom depends on the market, and is not simple at all. Witness some figures from filling stations in Minnesota—the E85 capital of America—in early [2005]. The pump price of the E10 gasoline standard in that state varied little, from around $1.90 a gallon to $2.10. E85 prices varied more, from about $1.50 to $1.80. And the gap between the two varied wildly: 26 cents in Austin, 34 in Owatonna, 45 in Eagan and Shakopee, 50 in Redwood Falls, 58 in Alden.

Say, typically, 35–45 cents and what the figures show is again simple, and conclusive: at today's [2005] prices, in that corn state, the wise driver buys subsidised E85 ethanol if he can; and it is only 10 cents or so from being cheaper than standard gasoline even were there no subsidies at all.

Other obstacles may be on the way out. Even now, a new flex-fuel car costs barely more than a standard one. There is little reason for any real differential, and as these cars gain popularity there may be none—as in Minnesota already. Guarantees have been a trouble: John Doe and his Chevy are past caring, but would you buy a brand-new car and risk invalidating its guarantee by using E85? But the car makers' attitudes are changing.

Guarantees are especially relevant to America's infant biodiesel industry. A heavy truck or combine harvester is a big investment to put at risk. But Case, a leading farm-equipment maker recently extended its guarantees to B5 (and at another, John Deere, machines leave the factory filled with B2). Volkswagen has just done likewise, as it and others did long ago in Europe, for its diesel-engined cars, a rare species in America, but now spreading.

American output of biodiesel is still trivial: [in 2004,] 30m gallons, in a total on-road diesel consumption of 36 billion. [In 2004], biodiesel cost about 20–30 cents a gallon more than petro-diesel. But ... a new law gave it too a federal tax credit: one cent for every 1% of biodiesel in the mix. Oil prices are higher now. And new rules requiring diesel in 2006 to be all-but-free of sulphur will help. Taking the sulphur out makes the fuel less slippery; adding biodiesel can make it more so.

Biodiesel Leader in Europe

The story has been much the same in Europe, though the leader there is biodiesel. In Germany, where more than half of all cars are diesel-engined, pure biodiesel, retailed as such, has long escaped fuel tax. In January 2004 blends up to B5 were legalised, and the exemption was extended, pro rata, to them. Per "biolitre", it is now worth euro 0.47 (in American terms, $2.30 a gallon). Italy takes off 40 euro-cents, France 33 (though both governments set a quota for output), Spain and Britain 29.

The public hears little of these tax breaks: in Germany or in France—where pure biodiesel is not sold—the driver looking for "diesel" seldom knows, or cares, that he may be getting B5. And even in Germany the pure stuff is available at only one filling-station in ten, thanks to the hostility of the oil companies. But where it is, drivers are eager for it: it is 10–12 euro-cents a litre cheaper than plain diesel. Big users buy in bulk, to blend for themselves at whatever percentage they like. And demand from the oil companies, since blending was authorised, has given Germany's biodiesel producers a huge boost.

Go, diesel, go!

| "We think we can drive the 'leanness,' or efficiency, of . . . gasoline to unheard-of levels."

Plasma Technology Can Improve Fuel Efficiency

Kevin Roark

In the following article, Kevin Roark describes a scientific project underway at the Los Alamos National Laboratory in New Mexico that uses an experimental plasma technology to improve gasoline efficiency in existing internal combustion engines. This approach—improving the fossil fuel the world runs on instead of developing an alternative renewable energy source—has vast cost-saving implications, according to Roark, and could not only make it possible for automobiles to meet stricter emissions standards but reduce harmful gas emissions to negligible levels. Kevin Roark is a spokesman for the Los Alamos National Laboratory, which conducts research in defense, energy, and environmental matters for the federal government.

As you read, consider the following questions:

1. How is gasoline transformed into a plasma, according to Roark?

Kevin Roark, "Plasma Combustion Technology Could Dramatically Improve Fuel Efficiency," www.lanl.gov, December 22, 2003. Copyright © 2003 UC. Reproduced by permission of the author.

2. Why is plasma fuel more efficient than untreated gasoline, according to the author?

3. What safety advantage would diesel engines have, in Don Coates's view, as quoted by Roark?

Imagine a jet engine able to cleanly burn cheap, plentiful diesel fuel, or a car able to run on gasoline very efficiently and produce practically no emissions. Three Los Alamos National Laboratory researchers are imagining just these things and are embarking on a new experimental roadway that may someday arrive at this reality.

The technology, a plasma combustion technique that applies electrical voltage to the gaseous-phase fuel stream prior to combustion—turning the fuel into a plasma—has already produced excellent results with propane. The next step, according to the research team, [composed of] Don Coates, an intellectual property and industrial partnerships coordinator with the Physics and Chemistry divisions, Louis Rosocha of the Plasma Physics Group and David Platts of the Hydrodynamics and X-ray Physics Group, is to move into a new experimental phase with a working fuel-injected gasoline engine.

But with no suitable engine readily available at the Laboratory, and no funding to purchase a new engine, the researchers were at an impasse. That's when Coates turned to the New Mexico vendor community. He quickly contacted Chris Tornillo at the Albuquerque branch of [diesel-engine maker] Cummins Rocky Mountain. "Chris recognized the value of the research almost at once," said Coates. "The Laboratory has had a wonderful working relationship with Cummins Rocky Mountain for years and so before too long he had offered to loan us, no strings attached, a brand-new Cummins generator engine that we could use for whatever research was needed—he said we could do whatever we wanted to it— obviously this level of generosity is pretty overwhelming." . . . "We can't wait to get started on the next set of experiments,"

Plasma Technology

The microplasmatron fuel converter (plasmatron, winner of the 1999 Discover Award for Technological Innovation) is a device that would be used on a vehicle to transform gasoline or other hydrocarbons into hydrogen rich gas. . . . The small size and rapid response of the plasmatron make it suitable for onboard vehicles. There is also a need to reduce air pollution from cars, trucks and buses . . . [and] to better use a greater variety of fuels to reduce greenhouse gas production and to conserve nonrenewable energy resources. Use of the plasmatron will provide a means to meet these needs at acceptable cost and without the requirement to reduce vehicle range and performance.

MIT Plasma Science and Fusion Center, "Plasma Technology," 2006.

said Coates. "We think we can drive the 'leanness,' or efficiency, of the gasoline to unheard of levels, much in the same way we did with propane."

Kerosene, propane, gasoline and diesel fuel are all hydrocarbons, all made up of the same basic chemical constituents but separated by the size of their individual molecules. The more efficient fuels, and therefore more highly refined and expensive, kerosene and propane, consist of fairly small chains of carbon and hydrogen atoms, whereas the less efficient and cheaper fuels, gasoline and diesel, are made of long chains of molecules. According to Coates, when electrodes attached at the spray nozzle of a fuel injector apply enough voltage to the fuel, energetic plasma electrons from voltage-induced breakdown of the fuel cause reactive species to be created, changing the basic chemical composition as the fuel becomes a plasma.

"You put into an engine the equivalent of a 'process plant' or fuel refinery," said Coates. "The plasma unit basically acts like a 'cracker' in a refinery, cutting the long chains of hydro-carbons into bite-size parts—the smaller the parts the better the burn—taking cheap fuels and making them combust like expensive ones."

Applying the Technology to Real Engines

The three researchers also believe they can construct a device that is relatively simple, cheap and easy to retrofit to existing fuel injection systems. "The ultimate goal is driven by fuel ef-ficiency, of course," said Coates. "But this could also have a dramatic impact on the environment, with the reduction of combustion waste products, specifically nitrogen oxide. In the coming years, new federal requirements will force internal combustion engines to be cleaner and cleaner—this technol-ogy could be one way to achieve compliance with the regula-tions. And when you think of things like large jet engines run-ning on diesel, there is a safety improvement as well; diesel will not explode like kerosene or gasoline, it's low flash-point makes it much more safe to use."

Periodical Bibliography

The following articles have been selected to supplement the diverse views presented in this chapter.

Steven Ashley   "On the Road to Fuel-Cell Cars," *Scientific American*, March 2005.

Donald L. Bartlett and James B. Steele   "Asleep at the Switch: Why America (but Not Canada) Failed to Set Up a Needed Synfuels Industry," *Time*, October 13, 2003.

Catalyst   "Hydrogen Fuel Cells," Spring 2004.

Jonathan Eisenthal   "Corn Bred to Fuel America," *EthanolToday*, March 2005.

FastCompany   "On the Road to Hydrogen," December 2004.

Fuel Cell Today   "Honda FCX Becomes Japan's First Fuel Cell Vehicle to Receive Motor Vehicle Type Certification," June 17, 2005.

Hydrogen and Fuel Cell Letter   "Fast Forward: Fuel Cell Train," October 2005. www.hfcletter.com.

Corinna Kester   "Diesels Versus Hybrids: Comparing the Environmental Costs," *World Watch*, July/August 2005.

Ben Lieberman   "Keep Ethanol Out of the Energy Bill," Heritage Foundation WebMemo #713, April 8, 2005. www.heritage.org/.

Jason Mark   "In the Driver's Seat," *Catalyst*, Fall 2004.

Jeanne Miller   "Biofuels: The Ultimate in Recycling," *Odyssey*, April 2004.

For Further Discussion

Chapter 1

1. Matthew Simmons maintains that cheap and accessible oil reserves are already in steep decline and predicts grave, global economic and political consequences. Conversely, Daniel Yergin contends that technological innovation will enable oil companies to discover more reserves and extract the earth's remaining oil more efficiently, and thus the world's oil supply is actually going to increase by 20 percent by 2010. Do you think fears of imminent fossil-fuel depletion are exaggerated? Explain your answer.

2. Goodstein's argument presumes that alternative energy sources are capable of replacing fossil fuels in the near future. Paul Roberts maintains to the contrary that *no* alternative energy source can compete with fossil fuels in performance or cost, that the cost of dismantling the existing petroleum-based global economy is incalculable, and that a transition to renewable energy is simply wishful thinking. Is Roberts's argument credible, in your opinion? If not, how does Roberts fail to support his assertions?

3. The Institute for the Analysis of Global Security argues that buying imported oil not only makes the United States economically dependent on foreign producers but puts money in the hands of anti-American political regimes that fund anti-American terrorism with U.S. dollars. In the authors' view, reducing foreign oil imports is thus in the interest of national security. Justin Fox disagrees, maintaining that depleting domestic oil resources would only make the United States more vulnerable both politically and economically, and the most prudent strategy is to buy cheap Middle East oil as long as it lasts. Which of these strategies do you feel best strengthens national security? Explain your answer.

Chapter 2

1. John Ritch pragmatically argues that an alternative to fossil fuels must be developed to sustain human activity on the planet and there is no better alternative than nuclear power. Helen Caldicott disputes nuclear-power advocates' claims that nuclear energy is clean or safe and insists that the risks of nuclear power far outweigh the benefits. In deciding which argument is more persuasive, compare and contrast both authors' specialized but different knowledge and experience. In what ways might Ritch's position as director-general of an international organization of nuclear power producers make his basic argument more or less credible? In what ways might Caldicott's profession as a physician make her argument more or less credible?

2. Patrick Moore was an environmental activist and staunch opponent of nuclear power in the 1960s and 1970s. Today the environmental movement is divided over the use of nuclear power, and Moore is one of several who have revised their opinion and now consider nuclear power a viable alternative energy source. Harvey Blatt is an environmentalist who reaches the opposite opinion; in his view, the record shows nuclear power plants have not been operating safely and seriously harm human health as well as the environment. Do you think an effective environmental movement should be unified on this issue, and if so, which position should it take? Support your opinion with evidence presented by Moore and Blatt.

3. Debate over the storage of nuclear waste usually focuses on the enormous length of time wastes remain radioactive, often measured in tens to hundreds of thousands of years and the challenges of ensuring its stability for such long periods. Matthew Wald and Mary Olson take different approaches to this issue: Wald suggests that devising a short-term solution, aboveground storage for fifty to a hundred years, is better than dithering over long-term so-

lutions whose safety is impossible to predict accurately. Olson concludes, in contrast, that nuclear waste cannot be stored safely anywhere, and thus nuclear energy is simply not a viable alternative energy source. Which author do you think makes the more persuasive argument? Why?

Chapter 3

1. Glenn Hamer characterizes solar energy as clean, efficient, and cost-effective. Michael Fox disputes solar industry claims, however, maintaining that even if solar, or photovoltaic (PV), cells could be produced for free, the costs of financing, installation, repair, maintenance, and replacement exceed the value of the electricity they can produce. Based on evidence presented in both viewpoints, do you feel solar energy should be pursued as an alternative energy source?

2. Jim Motavalli promotes the development of offshore "wind-farms" as an alternative energy source that could offset a projected natural gas supply shortage of 3 to 4 billion cubic feet per day. Eric Rosenbloom does not dispute the *potential* energy output of wind-powered generators, but argues that in reality, wind patterns fluctuate too much to make wind power reliable and people will not tolerate such wind systems' large, noisy presence in their community. Weigh the benefits and drawbacks of wind power presented in Motavalli's and Rosenbloom's articles and decide whether wind power should be pursued as an alternative energy source.

3. The U.S. Department of Energy promotes biomass—any plant-derived organic matter such as wood, plants, residue from agriculture or forestry, and the organic component of municipal and industrial wastes—as a renewable energy source and alternative to petroleum-based fuel. The National Geothermal Collaborative argues that the earth's own heat is a vast, untapped energy source. And the Na-

tional Economic Council contends that the best energy policy would encompass a wide range of alternative energy sources, variously applied where they will be most efficient. Debate the relative merit of these lesser-known alternative-energy technologies and decide which you would be willing to allocate tax dollars to research-and-development funding.

Chapter 4

1. Researchers estimate that some 400,000 hybrid vehicles— equipped with gasoline-powered engines supported by an electric motor during acceleration, such as the Toyota Prius and the Honda Insight—will be sold in the United States by 2007. David Friedman applauds this trend, citing hybrid vehicles as an important way to reduce oil consumption and even in the worst case an effective interim solution until gasoline-free vehicles can be brought to market. Kevin Roark considers plasma technology a better solution and advocates improving the fossil fuel the world runs on instead of developing an alternative renewable energy source. Based on evidence presented in Friedman's and Roark's viewpoints, do you think the goal of reducing oil consumption is best reached by improving gasoline efficiency or developing vehicles powered by alternative energy sources? Why?

2. Tom Nicholls examines vehicles powered by hydrogen, touted by advocates as a nearly perfect alternative to gasoline that actually releases more energy than it consumes. David W. Keith and Alexander E. Farrell present a different picture of hydrogen-powered vehicles, however, citing significant disadvantages such as high cost and difficulty of transport and storage. Consider the benefits and drawbacks of hydrogen power given by Nicholls, Keith, and Farrell. Do you feel the obstacles to the development of this alternative energy source are primarily technological or commercial? Explain your answer.

Organizations to Contact

Alliance to Save Energy
1200 Eighteenth St., Suite 900, Washington, DC   20036
(202) 530-2252
e-mail: acarmichael@ase.org
Web site: www.ase.org

The Alliance to Save Energy promotes energy efficiency world-wide to achieve a healthier economy, a cleaner environment, and greater energy security. To achieve this goal, the alliance leads worldwide energy-efficiency initiatives in research, policy advocacy, education, technology deployment, and communications.

American Council for an Energy-Efficient Economy (ACEEE)
1001 Connecticut Ave. NW, Suite 801
  Washington, DC   20036
(202) 429-8873 • fax: (202) 429-2248
e-mail: info@aceee.org
Web site: www.aceee.org

ACEEE's goal is to develop, analyze, advocate, and support the implementation of new policies for increasing energy efficiency in the United States. As part of its commitment to making energy efficiency the centerpiece of America's energy policy, ACEEE develops specific energy efficiency policy initiatives; analyzes their impacts; advises national, regional, and state policy makers; and works with coalitions of environmental, consumer, business, and progressive energy organizations. ACEEE actively participates in the energy policy, clean air, and climate change debates, developing policy recommendations and documenting how energy efficiency measures could reduce energy use, air pollutant emissions, and greenhouse gas emissions while benefiting the economy. The organization helps to develop and support energy efficiency programs sponsored by the U.S. Department of Energy (DOE) and Environmental Protection Agency (EPA).

American Council on Renewable Energy (ACORE)
1825 I St. NW, Suite 400, Washington, DC   20006
(202) 429-2030 • fax: (202) 429-5532
e-mail: meckhart@acore.org
Web site: www.acore.org

ACORE works to bring all forms of renewable energy into the mainstream of America's economy and Americans' private life.

California Wind Energy Consortium
Department of Mechanical and Aeronautical Engineering, Davis, CA   95616
(530) 752-7741 • fax: (530) 752-4158
http://flight.engr.ucdavis.edu/~cvandam

The consortium leads the development of safe, reliable, environmentally sound, and affordable wind electric generation capacity in the United States.

Consumer Federation of America (CFA)
1424 Sixteenth St. NW, Suite 604, Washington, DC   20036
(202) 387-6121
Web site: www.consumerfed.org

CFA is an advocacy, research, education, and service organization that works to advance pro-consumer policy on energy-related issues before Congress, the White House, federal and state regulatory agencies, state legislatures, and the courts.

Earth Policy Institute
1350 Connecticut Ave. NW, Suite 403
   Washington, DC   20036
(202) 496-9290 • fax: (202) 496-9325
e-mail: epi@earth-policy.org

The Earth Policy Institute was founded in 2001 to promote an environmentally sustainable economy.

The Energy Foundation
1012 Torney Ave. #1, San Francisco, CA   94129
(415) 561-6700 • fax: (415) 561-6709
Web site: www.ef.org

The foundation's mission is to assist in the nation's transition to a sustainable-energy economy by promoting energy efficiency and renewable energy sources. It functions primarily as a grant maker, but also sponsors workshops, publishes position papers, and participates in other direct initiatives.

Environmental News Service (ENS)
e-mail: news@ens-news.com
Web site: www.ens-newswire.com

This international daily newswire is an environmental news service for the latest news on the environment, current issues, climate, water, food, forests, species, and education. Includes an index and search tools.

International Solar Energy Society (ISES)
Wiesentalsr. 50, Freiburg   79115
  Germany
+49-761-45906-0 • fax: +49-761-45906-99
e-mail: hq@ises.org
Web site: www.ises.org

ISES is an international clearinghouse center for information on research and development in solar energy utilization. Through its publications and its sponsorship of technical conferences, the society provides a world forum for the active consideration of solar energy.

National Hydropower Association
One Massachusetts Ave. NW, Suite 850
  Washington, DC   20001

(202) 682-1700 • fax: (202) 682-9478
e-mail: help@hydro.org
Web site: www.hydro.org

The National Hydropower Association is the only national trade association dedicated exclusively to representing the interests of the hydropower industry.

Nuclear Energy Institute (NEI)
1776 I St. NW, Suite 400, Washington, DC   20006-3078
(202) 739-8000
e-mail: webmasterp@nei.org

NEI fosters the continued safe utilization and development of nuclear energy to meet the nation's energy, environmental, and economic goals and to support the nuclear energy industry.

Renewable and Appropriate Energy Laboratory (RAEL)
4152 Etcheverry Hall, Department of Nuclear Engineering,
   Berkeley, CA   94720
(510) 643-2243
e-mail: alove@berkeley.edu
Web site: http://ist-socrates.berkeley.edu/~rael/contact.html

RAEL publishes reports on the international application of renewable energy resources.

Renewable Energy Policy Project (REPP) and Center for Renewable Energy and Sustainable Technology (CREST)
1612 K St. NW, Suite 202, Washington, DC   20006
(202) 293-2898 • fax: (202) 293-5857
Web sites: www.repp.org, http://soltice.crest.org

A joint service offering information, insightful policy analysis, and innovative strategies for alternative-energy use amid changing energy markets and mounting environmental needs. REPP and CREST host ongoing online, renewable-energy discussion groups.

Resources for the Future
1616 P St. NW, Washington, DC   20036
(202) 328-5000 • fax: (202) 939-3460
Web site: www.rff.org

Materials available to the public from this nonprofit think tank include research papers on energy, electricity, and climate change; environment and development; environmental management; food and agriculture; natural and biological resources; technology and the environment; public health and the environment.

Union of Concerned Scientists (UCS)
Two Brattle St., Cambridge, MA   02139
(617) 547-5552
Web site: www.ucsusa.org

The Union of Concerned Scientists is an independent, nonprofit alliance of more than one hundred thousand concerned citizens and scientists. The union is an influential source of information on global warming, energy issues, scientific integrity, alternative vehicles, nuclear energy and other issues through several publications and its Web site.

U.S. Department of Energy (DOE)

The federal cabinet responsible for the development of U.S. energy policy and management of energy resources offers several Web sites for researchers, students, and the general public:

Energy Efficiency and Renewable Energy
www.eere.energy.gov

Archive of thousands of documents on renewables and conservation.

Energy Information Administration
www.eia.doe.gov

This comprehensive site provides detailed statistics about energy use and production.

Federal Energy Management Program
www.eere.energy.gov/femp

Promotes energy efficiency and the use of renewable energy resources at federal sites to help agencies save energy and save taxpayer dollars.

National Wind Technology Center
www.nrel.gov/wind

The National Wind Technology Center, located at the foot of the Rocky Mountains near Boulder, Colorado, is a world-class wind-power research facility managed by the National Renewable Energy Laboratory for the U.S. Department of Energy.

U.S. Department of Energy (DOE)
National Renewable Energy Laboratory
  Golden, CO   80401-3393
Web site: www.nrel.gov

NREL is DOE's primary laboratory for renewable energy and energy efficiency research and development. NREL's Hybrid Electric and Fuel Cell Vehicles research supports the U.S. Department of Energy's FreedomCAR & Vehicle Technologies Program.

World Nuclear Association (WNA)
Carlton House, 22A St. James Square, London   SW1Y 4JH
  England
+44(0) 20-7451-1520 • fax: +44(0) 20-7839-1501
Web site: www.world-nuclear.org

Seeks to promote the peaceful worldwide use of nuclear power as a sustainable energy resource for the coming centuries. Specifically, the WNA is concerned with nuclear power generation and all aspects of the nuclear fuel cycle, including mining, conversion, enrichment, fuel fabrication, plant manufacture, transport, and the safe disposition of spent fuel.

Bibliography of Books

Donald W. Aiken   *Transitioning to a Renewable Energy Future.* Freidburg, Germany: International Solar Energy Society, 2003.

American Wind Energy Association   *Wind Power Outlook 2005.* Washington, DC: American Wind Energy Association, 2005.

Robert Bent, Lloyd Orr, and Randall Baker, eds.   *Energy: Science, Policy, and the Pursuit of Sustainability.* Washington, DC: Island, 2002.

Paula Bernstein   *Alternative Energy: Facts, Statistics, and Issues.* Westport, CT: Oryx, 2001.

Harvey Blatt   *America's Environmental Report Card: Are We Making the Grade?* Cambridge, MA: MIT Press, 2004.

Lester R. Brown   *Eco-Economy: Building an Economy for the Earth.* New York: Norton, 2001.

Rex A. Ewing   *Power with Nature: Solar and Wind Demystified.* Masonville, CO: Pixyjack, 2003.

David Friedman   *A New Road: The Technology and Potential of Hybrid Vehicles.* Cambridge, MA: Union of Concerned Scientists, 2003.

Natale Goldstein   *Earth Almanac: An Annual Geophysical Review of the State of the Planet.* Westport, CT: Oryx, 2002.

Daniel M. Kammen, Kamal Kapadia, and Matthias Fripp
Putting Renewables to Work: How Many Jobs Can Clean Industry Generate? Berkeley: University of California, Energy and Resources Group, Goldman School of Public Policy, 2004.

Richard D. Morgenstern and Paul R. Portney, eds.
New Approaches on Energy and the Environment: Policy Advice for the President. Washington, DC: Resources for the Future, 2004.

Jeremy Rifkin
The Hydrogen Economy: The Creation of the Worldwide Energy Web and the Redistribution of Power on Earth. New York: Tarcher/Putnam, 2002.

Paul Roberts
The End of Oil: On the Edge of a Perilous New World. Boston: Houghton Mifflin, 2004.

John Schaeffer
Gaiam Real Goods Solar Living Sourcebook: Your Complete Guide to Renewable Energy Technologies and Sustainable Living. Ukiah, CA: Gaiam Real Goods, 2005.

James Gustave Speth, ed.
Red Sky at Morning: America and the Crisis of the Global Environment. New Haven, CT: Yale University Press, 2004.

James Gustave Speth, ed.
Worlds Apart: Globalization and the Environment. Washington, DC: Island, 2003.

Energy Alternatives

Vijay V.
Vaitheeswaran

_Power to the People: How the Coming
Energy Revolution Will Transform an
Industry, Change Our Lives, and
Maybe Even Save the Planet._ New
York: Farrar, Straus & Giroux, 2003.

55

Index